# Workers and Workplace Dynamics in Reconstruction-Era Atlanta:

## A  C A S E  S T U D Y

Afro-American Culture and Society
A CAAS Monograph Series
Volume 10


Center for Afro-American Studies, UCLA
Claudia Mitchell-Kernan, General Editor

# Workers and Workplace Dynamics in Reconstruction-Era Atlanta:

## A CASE STUDY

BY

## Jonathan W. McLeod

Center for Afro-American Studies
Institute of Industrial Relations
University of California, Los Angeles

Library of Congress Cataloging in Publication Data

McLeod, Jonathan W.
   Workers and workplace dynamics in Reconstruction-era Atlanta:
   a case study

   (Afro-American culture and society, ISSN 0882-5297; v. 10)
   Bibliography: p.
   Includes index
   1. Labor and laboring classes—Georgia—Atlanta—History—19th
century.   2. Industrial relations—Georgia—Atlanta—History—19th century.
3. Industrial sociology—Georgia—Atlanta—History—19th century.   4. Afro-
Americans—Employment—Georgia—Atlanta—History—19th century.
5. Sexual division of labor—Georgia—Atlanta—History—19th century.
I. Title.   II. Series: Afro-American culture and society; v. 10
HD8085.A783M35   1989        331'.09758'231—dc19         89-963
ISBN 0-934934-34-7


Center for Afro-American Sutdies
University of California, Los Angeles

Copyright © 1989 by The Regents
of the University of California

Second Printing 1991

Library of Congress Catalog Card Number 89-963
ISBN 0-934934-34-7
ISBN 0-89215-155-2
ISSN 0882-5297
Printed in the United States of America

*Design, Robin Weisz*
*Cover design, Rosalind Nzinga Vaughn*
*Produced by UCLA Publications Services Dept.*
*Typography, Freedmen's Organization*

# Acknowledgments

Grants for transportation, research, and writing from the Center for Afro-American Studies (CAAS) and the Institute of Industrial Relations (IIR) at the University of California, Los Angeles, were essential to my completing this monograph. CAAS Director Claudia Mitchell-Kernan and IIR Director Daniel Mitchell deserve special thanks. Also, I was the recipient of a travel award from the UCLA Chancellor's Patent Fund.

In utilizing sources, I benefited from the expertise of many librarians and staff workers at archives and libraries around the country. I acknowledge especially the assistance of the Reference and Inter-Library Loan Departments of UCLA's University Research Library. The aid of personnel at the Atlanta Historical Society, the Perkins Library of Duke University, the Robert W. Woodruff Library Special Collections Department of Emory University, the Georgia State Department of Archives and History, the National Archives and Records Administration, and the Library of the University of Georgia was invaluable.

Many people contributed time and energy to improve my study. Charles Cannon, Victor Cannon, Beth Falkins, Marcelle Fortier, Toni Lieteau, Jacqueline Tasch, Michael Toyoshima, and Jane Wildhorn offered their expertise in the preparation of the manuscript. I am grateful for the commentaries and sustained encouragement of David Brundage, Paul Bullock, George Cotkin, Margaret Washington Creel, Michael Fitzgerald, Paul Frisch, Judy Henson, Stephen Ray Henson, Robert McMath, Eric Monkkonen, Armstead Robinson, William Roy, Carole Srole, and Paul B. Worthman. I gained especially from my friendship with Robert W. Rydell and Alexander P. Saxton who graciously shared their scholarly expertise, made wise editorial suggestions, and spurred me on to complete this project.

My family, particularly my parents, Winifred and George McLeod, helped me immeasurably in bringing this study to fruition with their unfailing support. Nantawan Soonthorndhai McLeod, my spouse, offered critical insights and facilitated each step of this production. For her critical advice, technical assistance, and leap of faith, I am much indebted.

# Contents

# Introduction

Race, gender, and skill divisions affected workplace relations between Atlanta wage earners and their employers during the Reconstruction era. The impact shaped all aspects of life in the city throughout the last third of the nineteenth century. Focusing on Atlanta, this monograph extends southward the purview of nineteenth-century working-class community studies, which primarily have examined the more industrialized Northeast.[1] In so doing, it demonstrates the critical role the socially defined factor of race played in the history of American workers.

Founded in 1846, when it was designated the terminal of the Western & Atlantic Railroad, Atlanta developed differently from Northeastern urban centers. By 1860, the city had grown to approximately 10,000 residents, of whom some 2,000 were slaves. During the early 1860s, war-induced hardships drove many people in the hinterlands off their land and into urban areas. Consequently, in 1863, Atlanta's population grew to about 20,000. Soon thereafter, the forced evacuation of the city and its subsequent destruction by fire briefly displaced residents. Following the war, many returned to the ruins, where they were joined by newcomers. The 1870 census recorded some 22,000 residents, advancing Atlanta to eighth rank among the state's urban areas. A decade later, the number of inhabitants rose to 37,400, making Atlanta Georgia's fifth largest city.[2] Even as contemporaries boasted that the city had grown phoenix-like from the ashes of its wartime destruction, industrialization in Atlanta was not of the same magnitude as in urban centers of New York, Pennsylvania, and Massachusetts.[3]

While industrialization of Reconstruction-era Atlanta was of a comparatively lesser magnitude than that in the nation's leading urban centers, its effects were no less significant, as this was a city of workers. For wage earners in fast-changing Atlanta, as much as for Northern workers, job experiences were fundamental to ordering their lives. Gender divisions, the prestige of their respective occupations and their skill levels, as well as the nature of the work process, combined with employer paternalism to determine, in large measure, both relations between employers and wage earners and among fellow workers. Like their Northern counterparts, Atlantan wage earners were concerned with wages, conditions, and control of the workplace. At the same time, however, historians who have begun to investigate the lives of Southern workers have noted the particularly debilitating effect which racism had on their organizational efforts.[4] In Atlanta, where the working class was divided roughly equally between blacks and whites, disunity along racial lines exacerbated craft, occupational, and gender hierarchies.[5] The impact weakened the workers' responses to challenges confronting them as the Reconstruction era gave rise to the New South.

In probing the relations among workers and between the wage earners and their employers, the first chapter defines the parameters of Atlanta's economy overall. The second and third chapters present a close-up view of workplace dynamics in the city's main areas of employment—railroad, iron production, light manufacturing, food processing, construction, and service industries. Finally, this study concludes that by reinforcing craft, racial, and gender divisions which employers promoted through the work process, the workers impeded their own prospects for confronting their employers and restructuring the social relations of production.

## NOTES

1. Major studies of nineteenth-century Northeastern working-class communities include: Alan Dawley, *Class and Community: The Industrial Revolution in Lynn* (Cambridge and London: Harvard University Press, 1976); Daniel J. Walkowitz, *Worker City, Company Town: Iron and Cotton-Worker Protest in Troy and Cohoes, New York, 1855–84* (Urbana: University of Illinois Press, 1978); Paul G. Faler, *Mechanics and Manufacturers in the Early Industrial Revolution: Lynn, Massachusetts, 1780–1860* (Albany: State University of New York Press, 1981); Michael H. Frisch, *Town Into City: Springfield, Massachusetts, and the Meaning of Community, 1840–1880* (Cambridge: Harvard University Press, 1972); Bryan D. Palmer, *A Culture in Conflict: Skilled Workers and Industrial Capitalism in Hamilton, Ontario, 1860–1914* (Montreal: McGill-Queen's University Press, 1979); Clyde Griffen and Sally Griffen, *Natives and Newcomers: The Ordering of Opportunity in Mid-Nineteenth-Century Poughkeepsie* (Cambridge: Harvard University Press, 1978). Recently, some historians have begun to examine Midwestern and Western workers' communities. Notable among these monographs are: Steven J. Ross, *Workers on the Edge: Work, Leisure, and Politics in Industrializing Cincinnati, 1788–1890* (New York: Columbia University Press, 1985); Don Harrison Doyle, *The Social Order of a Frontier Community: Jacksonville, Illinois, 1825–1870* (Urbana: University of Illinois Press, 1978); David Brundage, "The Making of Working-Class Radicalism in the Mountain West: Denver, Colorado, 1880–1903" (Ph.D. dissertation, University of California, Los Angeles, 1982); Jules Everett Tygiel, "Workingmen in San Francisco, 1880–1901" (Ph.D. dissertation, University of California, Los Angeles, 1977); R. A. Burchell, *The San Francisco Irish, 1848–1880* (Berkeley: University of California Press, 1980); Joe William Trotter, Jr., *Black Milwaukee: The Making of an Industrial Proletariat* (Urbana and Chicago: University of Illinois Press, 1985).

2. Richard Joseph Hopkins, "Patterns of Persistence and Occupational Mobility in a Southern City: Atlanta, 1870–1920" (Ph.D. dissertation, Emory University, 1972), pp. 6–12.

3. Margaret Severence, *Official Guide to Atlanta* (Atlanta: Foote and Davies, 1895), p. 22; (Atlanta) *Daily New Era*, 26 October 1866; David R. Goldfield, *Cotton Fields and Skyscrapers: Southern City and Region, 1607–1980* (Baton Rouge and London: Louisiana State University Press, 1982), pp. 86–90, 120–26; Zane L. Miller and Patricia M. Melvin, *The Urbanization of Modern America: A Brief History* (San Diego: Harcourt Brace Jovanovich, 1987), pp. 34–38.

4. John M. Blassingame, *Black New Orleans, 1860–1880* (Chicago and London: University of Chicago Press, 1973); Peter J. Rachleff, *Black Labor in the South: Richmond, Virginia, 1865–1890* (Philadelphia: Temple University Press, 1984); David Paul Bennetts, "Black and White Workers: New Orleans, 1880–1900" (Ph.D. dissertation, University of Illinois, 1972); Dolores Elizabeth Janiewski, "From Field to Factory: Race, Class, Sex, and the Women Worker in Durham, 1880–1940" (Ph.D. dissertation, Duke University, 1979); James R. Green and Paul B. Worthman, "Black Workers and Labor Unions in Birmingham, Alabama, 1897–1915," in *Key Issues in the Afro-American Experience*, ed. Nathan Huggins et al. (New York: Harcourt Brace Jovanovich, 1971), 2:47–69; Stephen Ray Hensen, "Industrial Workers in the Mid Nineteenth-Century South: Atlanta Railwaymen, 1840–1870" (Ph.D. dissertation, Emory University, 1982).

5. Jerry John Thornbery, "The Development of Black Atlanta, 1865–1885" (Ph.D. dissertation, University of Maryland, 1977), p. 5.

# CHAPTER I

# Atlanta's Economy and Production Relations: an Overview

After the Civil War, workers of the Gate City functioned in a complex economy. In the interplay between institutional patterns and individual experience and consciousness, Atlanta's industrial and commercial base and the emergent social relations of production influenced the rhythms, forms, and content of the lives of workers and their families. Amid fluctuations in the nation's economy culminating in the depression of the 1870s, prosperity and security eluded most workers. Such conditions of economic flux and uncertainty of employment influenced the understanding of capitalism that workers acquired, intuitively or otherwise. This chapter defines the parameters of the local economy.

From the city's inception, railroading and its support industries formed the core of Atlanta's economy. As provided by the terms of the 1836 state charter enabling construction of a state railway, surveyors selected pristine land near the Chattahoochee River as the southern end of a rail line running to Chattanooga. Construction of this Western & Atlantic Railroad (W&A) began during 1837, slowly extending northward from the outpost, initially called Terminus, then renamed Marthasville and subsequently Atlanta. By 1851, workers completed construction of the W&A to Chattanooga.

That other rail lines soon converged on Atlanta further molded the character of the young city. During 1845, the Georgia Railroad reached Atlanta, followed in 1846 by the Macon & Western, which was absorbed subsequently by the Central of Georgia. Then, in 1853, service on the Atlanta & West Point commenced to Atlanta.[1]

As enterprises that not only kept the trains rolling, but also serviced the rolling stock and constructed and maintained the routes, these railroad companies rapidly emerged as principal industrial employers in Atlanta. During the antebellum period, several hundred workers of all skill levels held jobs on the several lines.[2]

Seeking to capitalize on the spectacular development of the railroad sector of the local economy, innovative Atlanta business leaders founded extensive complementary enterprises which diversified the local prewar economy. Principal among these was the foundry of Joseph Winship and Brothers, the largest manufacturing plant in Atlanta throughout the 1850s. Engaging some 40 workers, this enterprise specialized in construction and repair of railroad freight cars. The Atlanta Rolling Mill, established in 1858 under the proprietorship of Lewis Schofield and William Markham, employed an additional 100 workers, who rolled and rerolled rails and manufactured merchant bars.[3]

A variety of small-scale manufacturing establishments, which functioned in an auxiliary capacity to Atlanta's principal role as a railroad hub, rounded out the local antebellum economy. Such enterprises ranged from leather tanneries and a shoe factory to a sawmill and several furniture shops. They also included a flour mill, several makers of agricultural implements, and a few wagon-manufacturing establishments. Clothing factories engaged some seventy-five laborers. Meanwhile, a brewery, a whiskey distillery, and two cigar factories produced for the local market. Prewar Atlanta also boasted a printing and publishing house.[4]

The war changed the local economy. Cessation of trade with Northern industrial centers juxtaposed with the Confederate government's need for war material boosted the fortunes of Atlanta's manufacturing interests. The resultant activity pushed Atlanta into the ranks of major Confederate manufacturing and supply centers. Prominent among Confederate Atlanta's enterprises were a pistol factory and several brass and iron works, which produced arms and ammunition, along with accessories for uniforms and equipment. Shoe, match, soap, and candle factories engaged still more Atlantans in the manufacture of goods for the war effort. New competitors joined the established machine shops in producing cars and parts for the railroad, as well as weapons. Meeting the changed circumstances, operators of the Atlanta Rolling Mill retooled that plant for production of cannons and metal plating for ships, even as workers there continued to roll railroad tracks. Appropriately, in 1863, new owners temporarily changed the mill's name to the Confederate Rolling Mill.[5]

Within months of the 1864 fire that destroyed much of Atlanta, survivors and refugees shifted their attention to peacetime rebuilding. While allowance should be made for a high margin of error in figures on the size of the local labor force from the end of the war through 1880, in the interval between 1865 and 1870, the work force consisted of 4,000 to 5,000 male workers in all categories; approximately forty percent unskilled, thirty percent skilled, and the remaining thirty percent divided among white-collar workers, proprietors, and professionals.[6] Notably, statistics on women's labor-force participation are unreliable.

By 1880, the labor force expanded markedly. In manufacturing and mechanical industries alone, 4,198 Atlantans held jobs. Of these, 2,992 were males between the ages of sixteen and fifty-nine, and 925 were women of the same age cohort. At least 172 boys and girls from the ages of ten to fifteen worked in manufacturing establishments, as well.[7] Unfortunately, no reliable figure on the city's total labor force, inclusive of the trade, transportation, and service sectors, exists for 1880.

Not surprisingly, given the function of railroads in the local economy, the managements of the various railway companies moved swiftly following the war to repair, service, and restore those facilities, rolling stock, and equipment that survived the heavy use, minimal maintenance, and battle scars of the war years. All lines in the region had suffered significant damage inflicted by both the Confederate and Union armies. During combat, much of the rolling stock, as well as depots and repair shops, had burned. Under orders of General Sherman, in fact, Federal troops captured and effectively destroyed several entire railroads with the strategic goal of interrupting Confederate trade and supply routes.

By November 1864, for example, the Union Army took control of the W&A line, turning it over to the Union War Department in May 1865. In September 1865, ownership of the poorly maintained road reverted to the state government, which had originally owned it. At this point, workers speedily laid new rails and rebuilt bridges and terminals. (The W&A line remained under the direct control of the state until 1870. Then, dissenting factions of the Republican Party allied with John Emory Bryant charged Governor Rufus Bullock and Foster Blodgett with misadministration. Bullock then leased the road to private interests— ironically, to a company composed of Bullock's partners in affairs of government and boodle, Joseph E. Brown and Foster Blodgett.)[8]

While the state revitalized the W&A line, the other railroad companies with Atlanta operations initiated their own extensive rebuilding and repair programs using private capital. Competition for workers to

carry out the tasks was intense. For example, Aug Schwaab, of the Chief
Engineers' Office of the Central of Georgia Railroad, experienced frustration in recruiting a stable force of 400 to 450 laborers at low wages to
repair his company's tracks.[9]

Once full-scale service resumed, railroads traversing the city employed
hundreds of Atlantans, from laborers to engineers, who worked in the
repair shops, on road maintenance, and on moving trains. The com-
pletion in 1873 of yet a sixth rail line serving the city, the Atlanta &
Charlotte Airline Railroad, and the subsequent opening in 1878 of the
Airline car repair shops, further expanded local employment in that
industry.[10]

Considered as individual units, the companies operating local lines
varied considerably in size. Indeed, nationally, most railroad companies
hired fewer than 100 workers, and thereby fit the category of small industrial enterprises. Nonetheless, seventy-five percent of all railroad
workers across the country were on the payrolls of companies with 1,000
or more employees, which thus ranked among the nation's largest industries. As a case in point, 50,000 workers maintained and ran the Pennsylvania Railroad during the 1880s. Because payroll records for the
railroad companies operating in Atlanta during the period are only fragmentary, precise information on the full extent of such employment at
the local level is not available. One recent definitive study of railroad
workers has indicated that nationally about twenty percent of all such
employees until 1880 were shopmen. Projecting from one observation
that in 1866 the Georgia Railroad shop engaged 48 hands, while the
W&A hired 177 in its shop, it is reasonable to deduce that immediately
after the Civil War the Georgia Railroad functioned as a comparatively
small industrial operation, while the W&A classified as a medium-sized
industrial enterprise. Over time, employment on the railroads proved
critical to the local economy. Throughout the 1870s, in fact, the proportion of Atlanta workers engaged in transportation and trade enterprises
compared to those in manufacturing was higher than in other urban
areas.[11]

Recalling the importance of the Atlanta Rolling Mill to the late antebellum economy and eager for investment opportunities in the wake
of the war, several entrepreneurs pooled their capital to start a succes-
sor to the old mill the retreating Confederate Army had burned September 1, 1864. In March 1866, the Atlanta Mining and Rolling Mill
Company commenced operations, its capitalization amounting to

$400,000 by mid-1870.[12] Along with the railroad companies, this new mill company dominated the local economy and the local job market.

Within six months of starting operations, the mill employed more than 200. Moreover, at the peak of its activity in 1881 (before its destruction by fire late that same year), the labor force had expanded to approximately 500. By national standards, then, the mill ranked as a medium to large plant. Including dependents of its wage earners, the rolling mill's operations and policies immediately affected 1,000 to 2,000 Atlantans.[13] In that period, workers produced merchant bar iron, construction materials, castings for railroad-car wheels, and machine parts. Principally, however, the Atlantans rolled and rerolled rails for distribution throughout the South.[14]

Meanwhile, iron manufacturing in Atlanta, as across the nation, experienced sharp economic fluctuations. Overall in the South, the industry proved sluggish during the 1870s. According to Iron Molders' Union statistics, only fifty-four puddling furnaces operated in North Carolina, Georgia, Tennessee, and Alabama during that time. Just the expense of procuring those raw materials for production which were extracted elsewhere slowed expansion of iron and the introduction of steel manufacturing in the South until the 1880s. (During the 1880s, for the first time, mining of high-grade iron and coal deposits near Birmingham and Chattanooga sparked the expansion of iron and steel manufacturing in those cities.)

In effect, this problem undermined the Southern manufacturers' potential pricing advantage in commanding access to some other regionally available materials. Limited demand and the expense of reaching outlying markets with finished products further retarded these industries. During the 1870s, availability in the North of cheap iron and steel from highly efficient English and Scottish mills reinforced the competitive disadvantages Southern producers faced.[15] Finally, flagging demand, associated with the depression, weakened the iron and steel industries. Across the country, over one-third of iron foundries closed down by January 1, 1874. At those mills producing rails, like the Atlanta Rolling Mill, the situation was even more acute, with over half folding by that date.[16]

The mill in Atlanta was not immune to the effects of the depression, either. During June 1875, employees initiated a strike closing down the mill, after the management defaulted on paying $11,000 in back wages. In their own defense, the employers claimed other financial demands prevented the company from meeting its payroll obligations. Not surprisingly, perhaps, after the mill recommenced operations in 1876, it failed, and was successively placed in receivership and sold six times before the devastating fire in 1881. Even the respite for the iron industry between 1879 and 1880, when demand for iron outstripped the world supply, did not trigger a sustained recovery. During 1879 and 1880, employees at the Atlanta plant worked around the clock to fill orders; yet the mill still defaulted.[17]

Throughout this postwar period, numerous Atlanta entrepreneurs in medium-sized light industries also attempted to revive their own war-ravaged enterprises. Meanwhile newly arrived capitalists started medium-sized industrial ventures. Together these businesses broadened the city's economic base, while altering the residents' social relations. Prominent among such enterprises were a producer of agricultural implements, a planing mill, a hat manufacturer, and a cotton-spinning and bag factory.

Elias Haiman's Agricultural Implements Company (also known as the Southern Agricultural Works) typifies the medium-sized light manufacturing industries characteristic of Atlanta's economy, though this particular enterprise was larger than any of its competitors. Haiman, a practical mechanic and a farmer, had aided the Confederates during the war by supplying the troops with swords made in his plant. With the demise of the Confederacy, Haiman shifted into production of cultivators and plows, capitalizing his factory at $100,000. To meet the demand for his implements, Haiman employed an extensive force of workers of all skill levels. As a skilled worker himself, Haiman participated in both production and management.[18]

Operations at the city's largest planing mill, J. C. Peck and Company's Empire Steam Mill, followed a similar pattern. A crew of several dozen wage earners worked regularly with power-driven machinery, representing a considerable capital investment. Ultimately, the integration of skills at the plant yielded a steady output of doors, frames, sashes, blinds, and cabinet work.[19]

The straw factory of Jonas and Jacob Selig started during the 1870s and, in 1879, was restructured as the Selig and Sondheimer Sun Bonnet Factory (alternatively known as the Southern Sun Bonnet Factory) when A. Louis Sondheimer became a partner. It also numbered among the major medium-sized light industries in postwar Atlanta. By virtue of its $15,000 capitalization alone, the viability of this millinery factory influenced the stability of the local economy overall, generating substantial profits for the partners through the labor of several dozen workers.[20]

Finally, Atlanta's cotton textile mills warrant attention as medium-sized industrial concerns. Hannibal Ingalls Kimball's Atlanta Cotton Factory was the first to operate in the city. Kimball, a powerful and ambitious financier, started organizing his mill in 1875. Suspicions about his earlier postwar financial schemes and transactions that in 1871 had motivated him to depart the city hurriedly for Europe hung over Kimball on his return in 1874, clouding the prospects for the factory. Though newspaper accounts periodically announced 300 people had been hired to run the factory, protracted litigation against the management effectively stalled production.[21] Not until June 30, 1879, through the intervention of former Republican Governor Rufus Bullock (by 1879 reincarnated as a successful businessman and president of the Atlanta Chamber of Commerce), did the mill finally commence sustained operations. Local boosters again exulted that it "now works about 300 hands and consumes about twelve bales of cotton per day, making 15,000 yards of cloth." Promoters boasted of the mill's 20,000 spindles, a large number by Southern standards. Some 800 whites, they projected, soon would tend machines at the mill.[22]

Expectations for the cotton factory, however, languished. Wage earners there, three-fourths of whom were comparatively low-paid women and children, never numbered more than 500. Furthermore, Kimball quickly demonstrated that, during his earlier protracted absence from the state, he had not reformed his fund-raising and accounting practices. Fraudulent methods of organizing the cotton factory doomed it to failure.[23]

Other capitalists, nonetheless, were undeterred. In 1881, Jacob Elsas and Isaac May, owners of the Southern Bag Factory, purchased the charter granted to Kimball for the Atlanta Cotton Factory, which they reorganized as the Fulton Cotton Spinning Company. For its bag production during 1880, the company hired 100 to 160 men, women, and children.[24]

Another mill—the Exposition Cotton Mill Company—would open the following year, in 1882. That operation, under the management of F. P. Rice and R. H. Richards, took over facilities accommodating 20,000 spindles which the Willimantic Linen Company had erected for its exhibit at the International Cotton Exposition in Atlanta during 1881.[25]

In this postwar economy, Atlanta's few middle-sized manufacturing concerns differed from the multitudes of smaller-scale ones due to their variant patterns of labor-management relations and work organization.

Of course, these distinctions affected how individual workers perceived their world.

From the end of the war through the 1870s and beyond, small-scale enterprises competed actively, manufacturing a wide range of "producers' goods," as well as "consumer durables" and "consumer non-durables." Indeed, their proliferation and diversity reveal the importance of Atlanta's small-scale industries to the expanding local economy.

The common element linking these small industries—ranging from brickyards employing two skilled mechanics, to those having thirty wage earners, to furniture factories with seventy employees—remains the nature of labor-management relations governing them. Such establishments operated with minimal division of labor. Workers, therefore, generally related to one another on the job as parts of integral units. Meanwhile, employers cultivated personal relationships with wage earners, often enhanced by their laboring side-by-side. This work situation characterized much of the Atlanta economy at the time, contrasting with that of railroad and rolling-mill workers, and even with that of employees at such medium-sized plants as Kimball's Atlanta Cotton Factory.

John M. Smith and David McBride's carriage factory is a case in point. Starting their business in 1869 "in a small room on Decatur street," these two men had succeeded "solely on their own labor," the *Atlanta Constitution* noted in 1871. According to the newspaper, in two years of building carriages, they had expanded their operations to a level necessitating their employing twenty-three skilled production workers. Several years later, the *Constitution* again lauded Smith, observing that "he commenced work at his bench, and grew into a proprietor of [sic] slow but sure steps."[26]

Operations at the Central Planing Mill further exemplify this kind of relationship. Mr. Traynham, one of the partners owning the mill, had, prior to joining the ranks of the entrepreneurs, mastered the skills of a craftworker in a planing mill. By one account, even as an owner, Traynham regularly worked alongside fifty skilled saw and lathe operators and twenty-five additional skilled employees making doors, blinds, and sashes.[27]

Such a pattern prevailed in the smallest workshops engaged in outwork across the city, as well. Representative of these were the boot and shoe factories of W. E. Guthright and Marion Gaines, employing six and four workers respectively, and several cigar factories in individual residences.[28] In this latter form of factory organization, the small groups of workers and the proprietors functioned as distinct units, each being immediately dependent on the other groups in the chain of production. As close-knit production relations characterized many of Atlanta's manufacturing establishments, workers gained a more personalized perspective on their employers. Moreover, their employers' example of how upward mobility followed from hard work suggested to workers a model of harmonious labor-management relations.

The service sector also emerged as a central component of Atlanta's economy. The half-dozen local hotels early ranked among the city's largest employers of service workers. The Kimball House maintained an extensive staff for its steam laundry, bakery, restaurant kitchen, dining room, and other facilities, as well as for general maintenance. Operations at the Markham House Hotel also utilized porters and dining-room waiters.[29] An indeterminate number of employees operated the hospital administered by the Bureau of Refugees, Freedmen, and Abandoned Lands. Payroll records reveal that service workers staffing the hospital included nurses, kitchen and laundry workers, drivers, clerks, stewards, seamstresses, and laborers.[30] Other smaller-scale local enterprises also hired such wage earners, among them the Atlanta office of the Southern Express Company, the Atlanta Gas Company, several steam laundries, and no fewer than fifteen barber shops.[31] Moreover, a large proportion of working people participated in the service sector as individual entrepreneurs. Domestics, washerwomen, seamstresses, tailors, and small-restaurant proprietors fit this category. During 1869, some 150 men earned their livelihoods as dray operators.[32]

In ever larger numbers throughout the period, clericals entered the employ of local businesses and professional firms. Relocation of the state capital to Atlanta in 1868 generated additional demand for low-skilled secretaries to facilitate government operations. Similarly, the emerging complexity of manufacturing and commercial establishments triggered expansion in the ranks of office workers. By 1881, for example, the Singer sewing machine company's Atlanta agency employed women as bookkeepers and cashiers, as well as in other clerical positions. Likewise, the Bradstreet Commercial Agency staffed its office with ten female secretaries.[33]

Figures on clerical workers nationally provide a frame of reference for interpreting the case of Atlanta. In the United States during 1870, almost 77,000 workers had secretarial jobs; by 1880, this figure had grown to more than 500,000 or three percent of the nation's total labor force.

Assuming that Atlanta followed the trend of the country as a whole, particularly after becoming the seat of the state government in 1868, the clerical sector of the city's economy probably expanded rapidly between 1870 and 1880. Projecting from national statistics to the local level, four percent of the office workers in the latter year likely were female.[34] This represented a significant increase in the number of women so engaged over the preceding census year. The trend, of course, corresponded with changes altering the very nature of office work.

The expansive retail marketing sector in Atlanta stimulated employment of still more low-skilled workers as sales clerks. According to one contemporary, some 250 stores were located on the city's main business streets by 1866. Only five years later, he noted, that figure had increased to 400. Citywide, by 1871, 875 firms had obtained the obligatory operating licenses to commence business.[35] In keeping with the expansion in commercial enterprises, the number of sales workers, both male and female, expanded rapidly during the period. Prior to 1874, women sales clerks were confined solely to shops in which no males were employed, such as millinery stores. In 1874, the first woman was hired as a sales clerk to work alongside male workers. The trend continued until, by 1878, over 100 women worked with men in general dry-goods stores alone. The yardage shop of Regenstein and Kurtz in 1878 employed 30 clerks, two-thirds of whom were women. Two years later, according to a local newspaper, the number of workers at this shop had expanded to 35 women.[36]

In the face of the city's persistent economic crisis, increasing numbers of individuals entered the sales sector as street vendors. The volume of requests for vendor's licenses the city council received indicates the impact of the depression on Atlantans. On occasion, the council even waived license fees for indigent applicants.[37]

At the same time, blacks did not sustain an autonomous commercial economy set off by their "blackness." Nevertheless, in several lines, entrepreneurially inclined freedpeople defied the odds of limited access to credit and white competition, setting up their own service-sector ventures and employing black wage earners.

In conformity with the emerging postbellum pattern of racial segregation in intimate social relations, some of these black-owned/black-run service enterprises catered solely to whites. Barber shops, for example, served either an exclusively white or exclusively black clientele.[38] Most black workers in such black-owned businesses, however, served a somewhat more diversified clientele. In the mid-1870s, Crawford Monroe employed blacks to operate ten of the city's best drays. Other black service-worker/owners ran restaurants and "tawdry dives" whites patronized. Black wage earners also labored in black-owned groceries and dry-goods stores, in laundry and tailoring shops, and for undertakers.

A few of these enterprises thrived. Most, however, remained economically marginal while they persisted, a predictable outcome in the wake of the war and amid the depression of the 1870s. Capitalization in these black-owned service-sector enterprises remained low. Characteristically, owners and workers had close personal relations based on their common experience laboring side-by-side as service workers.[39]

Despite the persistent economic crisis, another sector of the local economy—the building trades—thrived during the early postbellum period. Physical destruction of the city during the war subsequently caused a boom in the construction industry. Moreover, newcomers arriving from the hinterlands and other urban areas increased demand for housing and commercial buildings. John Dennett, a Northern journalist traveling through the South immediately after the war, described the scene in Atlanta:

> The middle of the city is a great open space of irregular shape, a wilderness of mud, with a confused jumble of railway sheds, and traversed by numberless rails, rusted and splashed, where strings of dirty cars are standing, and engines constantly puff and whistle. . . . Bricks and blocks of stone and other rubbish were everywhere. Around this central square the city was formerly built, and is now again building. Unfinished houses are to be seen on every hand; scaffolding, mortar-boards, and lime-barrels, piles of lumber and bricks and mounds of sand, choke every street, and the whole place on working days resounds with the noise of carpenters and masons.[40]

Under these circumstances, at least skilled workers in the building trades enjoyed relative prosperity and regular employment. In surveying the economic structure of Atlanta, therefore, the construction industry warrants examination.

In 1866, the (Atlanta) *Daily New Era* estimated some 350 structures were under construction within the city. Four years later, in 1870, building-trades workers still benefited from the boom with as many as 500 construction projects underway throughout the city. In 1868, eight contracting companies sought operational permits in Atlanta; by 1870, that figure rose to fifteen.[41] Many of the construction-trades workers, of course, labored on small projects, restoring and outfitting homes and shops.[42] Yet, as a matter of course, a large proportion of these high- and low-skilled wage earners labored on larger projects, ranging from the construction of barracks for the United States Army troops stationed in Atlanta during 1868, to the erection of the Kimball House Hotel.[43] Carpenters and laborers anticipated steady work during 1870 in conjunction with the building of the state fair grounds.[44] Hundreds also found jobs in road work, such as building the turnpike from Atlanta to Stone Mountain.[45]

Such frenetic activity swelled the number of construction workers in 1870 to nearly 3,000 steady employees. Yet, such work was subject to sharp fluctuations. The demand for building-trades workers was so great that periodic shortages in particular crafts created bottlenecks in the whole industry. In other periods, as in 1867 when the ex-Confederates ceased all improvements on their properties in fear of congressional action to confiscate their lands, and during the height of the depression of the 1870s, the building industry slumped.[46]

In sum, the city's postbellum economic base was relatively diversified. Before and following the nationwide industrial depression of the 1870s, the local economy proved dynamic, though opportunity and the distribution of capital remained skewed. This economic vitality, in large measure, rested less on the extractive industries, which stimulated the economies of Pennsylvania, West Virginia, and Illinois, or on large-scale heavy manufacturing, which was beginning to typify emerging industrial centers of the Northeast, than on the transportation and service sectors of the economy.[47] Cotton mills operating in Atlanta early in the 1880s ranked among the major local employers and were among the largest such establishments in the state. Once Georgia's entrepreneurs and Northern investors began a textile mill boom in the 1880s, however, Augusta, Macon, and Columbus emerged as the preferred sites.[48] Ongoing industrial production in Atlanta generally was of a small- to medium-scale, involving secondary manufacturing, or that utilizing already finished parts. Machinists, for example, often used metal castings brought in from other sources. The local rolling mill remained a notable exception in producing primary goods, particularly rails. Operations in the transportation sector, in contrast, included a few large-scale enterprises, most significantly, the W&A Railroad. Service-sector employment in Atlanta also varied in scope, ranging from that in dry-goods stores, restaurants, and hotels to the individual enterprises of domestic workers, clericals, barbers, and small merchants, among others. The construction trades, as well, were structured variously, including self-employed building-trades workers and firms hiring hundreds of workers in various projects. This framework, then, formed the structure in which production relations in Reconstruction-era Atlanta unfolded.

## NOTES

1. Franklin M. Garrett, *Atlanta and Environs: A Chronicle of Its People and Events*, 2 vols. (Athens: University of Georgia Press, 1969), 1:150, 168, 232; F. N. Boney, "1820–1865," in *A History of Georgia*, ed. Kenneth Coleman et al. (Athens: University of Georgia Press, 1977), p. 159.

2. Henson, "Industrial Workers," pp. 39–40; Garrett, *Atlanta and Environs*, 1:359–60.

3. Grigsby Hart Wotton, Jr., "New City of the South: Atlanta, 1843–1873" (Ph.D. dissertation, Johns Hopkins University, 1973), pp. 29, 39–40; Garrett, *Atlanta and Environs*, 1:426–27.

4. Wotton, "New City," pp. 28–29.

5. Ibid., pp. 91–95; Garrett, *Atlanta and Environs*, 1:427.

6. (Atlanta) *Daily New Era*, 11 November 1866; Wotton, "New City," p. 218.

7. United States Census Office, *Tenth Census* (1880), vol. 2: *Report on the Manufactures of the United States* (Washington, 1883), p. xxxiii.

8. Garrett, *Atlanta and Environs*, 1:633–34, 649, 651, 710–11; Wotton, "New City," pp. 118–19; Western & Atlantic Railroad Company, *Annual Reports of the Officers of the Western & Atlantic Rail Road* (Atlanta: Atlanta Intelligencer Book and Job Office, 1866), pp. 18–19; Henson, "Industrial Workers," p. 184; Elizabeth Studley Nathans, *Losing the Peace: Georgia Republicans and Reconstruction, 1865–1871* (Baton Rouge: Louisiana State University Press, 1968), pp. 206–12.

9. Wotton, "New City," pp. 118–19; United States Army Continental Commands, Third Military District, Record Group 393, Letters Received by the Commander, Department of Georgia, letter from Aug Schwaab, 30 July 1865, National Archives and Records Administration, Washington (hereafter cited as NARA).

10. Garrett, *Atlanta and Environs*, 1:487, 895; *Atlanta Constitution*, 24 March 1878, 1 April 1880.

11. Thomas C. Cochran and William Miller, *Age of Enterprise: A Social History of Industrial America* (New York: Harper and Row, 1961), p. 230; *International Encyclopedia of the Social Sciences*, vol. 7 (n.p.: Crowell, Collier and Macmillan, 1968), pp. 270–72; Walter [Martin] Licht, *Working for the Railroad: The Organization of Work in the Nineteenth Century* (Princeton: Princeton University Press, 1983), p. 16; Licht, "Nineteenth-Century American Railwaymen: A Study in the Nature and Organization of Work" (Ph.D. dissertation, Princeton University, 1977), pp. 40–43; James Michael Russell, "Atlanta: Gate City of the South, 1847 to 1885" (Ph.D. dissertation, Princeton University, 1972), p. 152; Wotton, "New City," p. 219.

12. Garrett, *Atlanta and Environs*, 1:633–34, 712–13; (Atlanta) *Daily Intelligencer*, 3 June 1870.

13. *Atlanta Constitution*, 2 September 1868, 14 September 1873, 18 June 1879, 1 April 1880, 10 May 1881; (Atlanta) *Daily New Era*, 7 October 1871; (Philadelphia) *Textile Record*, 1881, p. 8; Cochran and Miller, *Age of Enterprise*, p. 230.

14. (Atlanta) *Daily New Era*, 3 November 1866; *Atlanta Constitution*, 14 August 1872, 10 May 1876; Wotton, "New City," pp. 175-76.

15. *Iron Molders' Journal*, 10 December 1875, p. 526; Kenneth Warren, *The American Steel Industry, 1850-1970: A Geographical Interpretation* (Oxford: Clarendon Press, 1973), p. 182; Russell, "Atlanta: Gate City," pp. 243-44; Gerald David Jaynes, *Branches Without Roots: Genesis of the Black Working Class in the American South, 1862-1882* (New York and Oxford: Oxford University Press, 1986), p. 286.

16. Herbert G. Gutman, "The Workers Search for Power," in *The Gilded Age*, ed. H. Wayne Morgan (New York: Syracuse University Press, 1970), p. 35; Daniel J. Walkowitz, *Worker City Company Town*, p. 11; Victor S. Clark, *History of Manufactures in the United States*, 3 vols. (New York: Peter Smith, 1949), 2:293.

17. *Atlanta Constitution*, 17 June 1875, 18 June 1879, 7 October 1879, 7 January 1881, 10 May 1881; Garrett, *Atlanta and Environs*, 1:712-13; *Beasley's Atlanta Directory for 1874* (Atlanta: Beasley and Company, n.d.), p. 299; *Sholes' Atlanta City Directory for 1877* (Atlanta: Sunny South Publishing House, n.d.), back paster; *Sholes' Directory for the City of Atlanta for 1881* (Atlanta: H. H. Dickson, n.d.), back fly D.

18. *Atlanta Constitution*, 22 September 1880; Steven Hertzberg, *Strangers Within the Gate City: The Jews of Atlanta, 1845-1915* (Philadelphia: Jewish Publication Society of America, 1978), p. 40; United States Bureau of the Census, Special Schedules of Manufactures of the Tenth Census of the United States, 1880, Georgia, Fulton County, not paginated, Manuscript Division, The Perkins Library, Duke University.

19. (Atlanta) *Daily Herald*, 1 November 1872.

20. Hertzberg, *Strangers Within the Gate City*, p. 40; Tenth Census, Special Schedules of Manufactures. For comparative figures on average capital investment in the North and nationwide, see David Montgomery, *Beyond Equality: Labor and the Radical Republicans, 1862-1872* (New York: Vintage Books, 1967), p. 13.

21. Garrett, *Atlanta and Environs*, 1:908-9; *Atlanta Constitution*, 29 January 1878; (Atlanta) *Methodist Advocate*, 6 February 1878.

22. Diary of Samuel P. Richards, vol. 13, 30 June 1879, Samuel P. Richards Collection, Atlanta Historical Society (hereafter cited as AHS); *Atlanta Constitution*, 19 September 1879, 7 October 1879; *New York Times*, 3 November 1881; Numan V. Bartley, *The Creation of Modern Georgia* (Athens: University of Georgia Press, 1983), p. 73.

23. *Atlanta Constitution*, 1 April 1880; Russell, "Atlanta: Gate City," pp. 158-61; Alice E. Reagan, *H. I. Kimball, Entrepreneur* (Atlanta: Cherokee Publishing Company, 1983), pp. 77-90.

24. Garrett, *Atlanta and Environs*, 1:808-9; Hertzberg, *Strangers Within the Gate City*, p. 40; *Atlanta Constitution*, 1 April 1880; Tenth Census, Special Schedule of Manufactures.

25. "The Mill That Began as a World's Fair," *Ties* (July 1962), p. 11; *New York Times*, 3 November 1881; *Atlanta Constitution*, 5 October 1881; Garrett, *Atlanta and Environs*, 2:41-42.

26. *Atlanta Constitution*, 24 December 1871, 22 September 1880.

27. Ibid., 7 October 1879.

28. Tenth Census, Special Schedule of Manufactures; *Atlanta Constitution*, 17 February 1872; Hertzberg, *Strangers Within the Gate City*, p. 41; (Atlanta) *Daily Intelligencer*, 17 June 1869.

29. John Stainback Wilson, *Atlanta As It Is: Being a Brief Sketch of Its Early Settlers, Growth, Society, Health, Morals, Publications, Churches, Associations, Educational Institutions, Prominent Officials, Principal Business Enterprises, Public Buildings, Etc., Etc.* (New

York: Little, Rennie & Co., 1871), [Reprinted as: *The Atlanta Historical Bulletin* 6, no. 24 (January and April 1941)], p. 66; *Atlanta Constitution*, 3 September 1878; (Atlanta) *Daily New Era*, 12 October 1870.

30. Extant monthly hospital records reflect an extensive turnover in the labor force; but no definitive totals on the size of the labor force throughout the period is included. United States Bureau of Refugees, Freedmen, and Abandoned Lands (hereafter cited as BRFAL), Retained Reports of Attendants Employed at the BRFAL Hospital, Atlanta, NARA, Record Group 105 (hereafter cited as RG 105); National Archives Microfilm Publications, Registers and Letters Received by the Commissioner, BRFAL (Washington, n.d.), Microcopy 752, Roll 49, Report of Employees, State of Georgia, 1 September 1867.

31. *Atlanta Constitution*, 15 April 1873, 28 October 1877; Tenth Census, Special Schedules of Manufactures; Wilson, *Atlanta As It Is*, p. 17.

32. *Atlanta Constitution*, 29 January 1869.

33. Wilson, *Atlanta As It Is*, p. 17; V. T. Barnwell, *Barnwell's Atlanta City Directory and Strangers' Guide* (Atlanta: Intelligencer Book and Job Office, 1867), pp. 34–35; *Atlanta Constitution*, 16 June 1881.

34. Margery Davies, "Women's Place Is At the Typewriter: Feminization of the Clerical Labor Force," *Radical America* 8, no. 4 (July–August 1974): 2, 3, 5; Elyce J. Rotella, "The Transformation of the American Office: Changes in Employment and Technology," *Journal of Economic History* 41, no. 1 (March 1981): 51–52.

35. Wilson, *Atlanta As It Is*, p. 17.

36. *Atlanta Constitution*, 27 March 1878, 1 April 1880.

37. Ibid., 16 January 1869, 7 December 1875; Atlanta, City Council Minutes, 28 July 1871, AHS.

38. Howard N. Rabinowitz, *Race Relations in the Urban South, 1865–1890* (Urbana: University of Illinois Press, 1980); *Atlanta Constitution*, 9 March 1875.

39. Rabinowitz, *Race Relations*, pp. 89–90; *Atlanta Constitution*, 2 February 1874, 28 December 1875, 28 July 1880, 20 July 1881.

40. John Richard Dennett, *The South As It Is: 1865–1866* (New York: Viking Press, 1965), pp. 267–68.

41. (Atlanta) *Daily New Era*, 26 October 1866, 7 May 1870; Atlanta City Clerk's Office, Register of Merchants, 1868–1870, AHS.

42. Samuel P. Richards Diary, vol. 12, 15 January 1873, 22 February 1873, 6 March 1873.

43. Arthur Reed Taylor, "From the Ashes: Atlanta during Reconstruction, 1865–1876" (Ph.D. dissertation, Emory University, 1973), p. 104; Wotton, "New City," p. 165; (Atlanta) *Daily New Era*, 17 May 1870.

44. (Atlanta) *Daily New Era*, 6 June 1870, 6 September 1870.

45. Ibid., 18 July 1871.

46. Taylor, "From the Ashes," p. 104; *Atlanta Constitution*, 1 April 1880; (Atlanta) *Daily New Era*, 2 July 1871; American Missionary Association, Archives, Georgia manuscripts microfilm publications, Roll 3, Letter 20617 to Rev. E. P. Smith, 30 March 1867.

47. Edward C. Kirkland, *Industry Comes of Age: Business, Labor, and Public Policy, 1860–1897* (New York: Holt, Rinehart and Winston, 1961), p. 141.

48. *Tenth Census, Report on the Manufactures* (1883), pp. 207–10; Charles E. Wynes, "1865–1890," in *A History of Georgia*, ed. Coleman et al., p. 235; Goldfield, *Cotton Fields and Skyscrapers*, pp. 123–24; Bartley, *The Creation of Modern Georgia*, p. 109; Gavin Wright, *Old South, New South: Revolutions in the Southern Economy Since the Civil War* (New York: Basic Books, 1986), p. 129.

# CHAPTER II

# RAILROADS

## AND

# IRON MILLS

As the nation industrialized, the social relations of workers with each other and with their employers on the job influenced how wage earners understood the work process. Of course, not all workers—even in a particular place—viewed their work experiences from a uniform perspective. In part, this reflected the unevenness of technological change, variations in the labor market, and the gradations of their positions in the occupational hierarchy.[1] Moreover, those working in postwar Atlanta came from many settings—including Atlanta's hinterland, Northern urban centers, and Europe—and, therefore, had differing occupational histories. Also, their varied backgrounds meant that Atlantans interpreted their work experiences through diverse ideologies. In the interplay between experience and intellectual reflection, however, workplace dynamics formed a critical context for workers' responses and initiatives.

To clarify the nature of interactions among wage earners in Atlanta, then, it is essential to examine their employment situations, observing the interpersonal dynamics in the work processes and the derivative social relations of production. In Atlanta's large-scale industries—railroading and iron manufacturing—the patterns of production relations that evolved in varying degrees institutionalized race, craft, and skill distinctions in the exclusively male labor force. Recognizing the advantages for management in controlling hundreds of employees in impersonal, hierarchical, and bureaucratized workplaces, employers furthered the historically rooted divisions among workers. Their efforts, the employers hoped, would defuse contrary tendencies toward working-class consciousness and collective action. Workers, responding to arbitrary managerial policies and exploitative patterns of production relations, differed on how best to advance their short- and long-term self-interests. Problems in forging solidarity to transcend structural divisions and to exercise power in the workplace, thus, posed a fundamental challenge. This chapter addresses laboring in Atlanta's large-scale industries: railroading and iron manufacturing.

## Railroads

Railroading was Atlanta's largest industry. Evolving patterns of ownership and administration, coupled with alterations in the mode of operations, affected the workers on the five lines passing through the city, when the managers attempted to achieve operational economy by modifying job processes and implementing modern managerial policies. The conflicts emergent among the affected workers, as well as between the employees and management, and the ultimate impact of these changes on the social relations of production in the industry are the subject of the present analysis.

### 1. Assembling a labor force

Once the siege of Atlanta lifted and control of the Western & Atlantic returned from the United States Army to the state government in September 1865, management assigned top priority to recruitment of a work force for replacing mangled tracks and repairing road beds and bridges. Competition for laborers intensified as other rail lines also sought workers to renovate their own physical plants and rolling stock. Work progressed rapidly so that, by the late spring of 1866, temporary wooden buildings housed shops of the W&A and the Georgia Railroad lines. Meanwhile, managers sought out skilled shop workers. Restoration of the rolling stock—much of which had been disassembled and shuttled around the state for safekeeping late in the war, together with that which had been damaged during the final siege—was a primary management concern. Once limited runs recommenced, servicing the engines and cars was vital, for operating conditions on most of those routes that were passable remained far from ideal.[2]

Such heavy demand for the skills and labor power of employees in the road and machinery departments of Atlanta's railroads did not carry over directly into the transportation departments. In the wake of extensive

*Atlanta & Charlotte Air Line R.R. No. 12*
Courtesy of the Atlanta Historical Society, Inc.

wartime damage, workers could repair the rail lines only gradually. Hampered by the limited capacities of the lines, trains moved on a restricted level. Consequently, employment for engineers, conductors, and support crews remained minimal, and only a portion of those working prior to and/or during the Civil War were able to secure jobs they had held previously.[3]

When operations returned to normal, employment on the W&A rose. During 1869, a monthly average of 742 train operators, service workers, and station personnel kept the W&A trains rolling, the actual figures climbing to 819 in July from an April low of 646.[4] The majority of employees (as on the other lines as well) were semiskilled and unskilled; the skilled workers in the road, machinery, and transportation departments formed an elite core.

Coincidental accusations of partisanship in the policies of the incumbent administration, which allegedly schemed to win black votes, abounded. According to the charges, Republican Governor Rufus Bullock and his appointees overseeing W&A employment, including United States Senator and General Henry P. Farrow and W&A Superintendent Edward Hulbert (1868), violated seniority in their flagrant misuse of patronage, padding the State Road's payroll with black Republicans while dismissing numerous experienced white railroad employees who were Democrats. The fact that by 1873, three years after having leased the W&A line, Joseph E. Brown operated the company with only 523 workers suggests that these allegations may have contained considerable validity.[5]

Throughout the period, black males comprised a significant number of the employees on all lines traversing the city. Statistics compiled from the 1870 and 1880 manuscript schedules of the population censuses, used in conjunction with an extant partial payroll of the W&A (dated 1865), reveal that in 1870, between 77 and 89 blacks held railroad jobs. Ten years later in 1880, upwards of 133 blacks worked in the industry. Yet, blacks never held railroad jobs in numbers commensurate with their proportion of the city's population. Moreover, few secured skilled positions, the majority being confined to semiskilled and unskilled jobs.[6]

## 2. Wages

Incomplete data allow only a qualified analysis of pay rates for the several classifications of Atlanta railroad workers. During the first two-thirds of 1865, engineers in the Atlanta Division of the W&A received from $7 to $12 as standard daily compensation, depending on rank. That was two to three times what they were to receive ten years later, when the standard daily rate hovered at $4.[7]

Significantly, however, W&A engineers did not share the even harsher plight of some of their Northern counterparts, who simultaneously suffered wage cuts and a change in the system of remuneration forcing still higher productivity. On the Illinois Central, for example, management imposed a piece-rate system on engineers. Under the new procedures, engineers received pay based on mileage covered, rather than the customary flat daily rate.[8] To their comparative advantage the Atlanta train crews contended principally with wage cuts.

In fact, during and after 1870, under Brown's management, all grades of W&A employees, including shop workers, faced drastic wage reductions. So harsh was the impact on the workers' standard of living—even as, overall, postwar deflation of consumer prices and slowly rising real wages eventually realigned income and the cost of living nationwide—that, in August 1872, writers for the (Atlanta) *Daily Herald* attacked Brown's policies. Criticizing the company for insensitivity to the hardworking, deserving workers, one account in that newspaper noted, "the pay they now receive is not more than sufficient to support themselves and their families and a further reduction will only result in depriving them of many comforts, if not of absolute necessities. Should the reduction be made," the newspaper concluded, "we shall unqualifiedly take the part of the workmen, because we do not believe there is any special necesity [sic] for further reduction by the lessees."[9]

If in opposing wage cuts, the railroad workers stood on common ground, the wide gaps in their earnings, as pegged to the occupational hierarchy, categorically separated the more skilled from the lower-order workers. Within their narrow craft-oriented spheres, W&A conductors and engineers, who in 1865 earned daily wages of $6.80 and $12 respectively, most likely had different concerns in the face of subsequent wage cuts from the lower-skilled train hands, who received $3.50 per day. The perspectives of the latter group of workers, in turn, undoubtedly differed fundamentally from those of track hands on the Atlanta & West Point, who commanded a mere $0.86 per day.[10]

Furthermore, despite a false security periodically induced by receiving wages due on schedule, the underlying tenuousness of all the railroad workers' jobs and their related economic vulnerability persistently dominated their lives. Fear of injuries on the job hung over them constantly.[11] Successive expansions and contractions of the local railroad labor force, corresponding with the seasonal handling of agricultural products and with the depression, also prompted labor-force turnover. Indeed, during the nineteenth century, (particularly before 1880), as few as half of the nation's railroad workers sustained employment in the trade.[12]

### 3. Skill division and the organization of job tasks

Distinctions among the railroad workers, which the hierarchical nature of the wage structure suggests, manifested themselves functionally on the job and in the emerging social relations of production. Railroad company operations, being organized in three departments (machinery, road, and transportation), functioned with an elaborate division of labor and an explicit chain of command.

Because tasks in the machinery division brought together so many craftworkers, the department had a diverse labor force. Indeed, from the mid-1850s, the volume of work dictated that each railroad company operating out of Atlanta organize the division in two units, a motive shop and a car shop. Wage earners in each were responsible to the shop supervisors and master mechanics, who routinely participated in the work process. These supervisors emerged, therefore, as the lowest level of management in the department, answering in turn to the general superintendent of transportation on business affairs.[13]

Tradeworkers in the motive shops, including machinists, boilermakers, coppersmiths, and blacksmiths, were expected to be proficient in all aspects of the repair and maintenance of locomotives. Significantly, through the 1860s, a substantial proportion of these workers were recruited from beyond Atlanta and its hinterland, reflecting the shortage locally of wage earners trained to use the most sophisticated machinery. Most who migrated there were U.S.-born whites, some having been trained in Philadelphia machine shops. Immediately after the war, some fourteen of twenty-eight machinists who had worked in Atlanta shops prior to the war returned to take up their trades anew. Whether they were holdovers or new arrivals, only thirteen of fifty-five machinists appearing in the 1870 census claimed foreign birth. Once again, then, the dependence of the railroad companies on Northeast machine shops for personnel continued the homogeneity of the labor force in that department.

Occasionally former slaves filled skilled positions in the postbellum motive shops. Augustus Thompson, born a slave in Jackson, Mississippi, exemplified this small group. Upon moving with his master to Georgia,

*Railroad Car Shops, Atlanta*
Courtesy of the Atlanta Historical Society, Inc.

he commenced an apprenticeship in blacksmithing, which led to his war-time engagement in the Confederate Gun Factory and the Augusta Machine Works. After the war, Thompson resumed blacksmithing and moved to Atlanta early in 1870. He found employment as a boilermaker in the W&A shops, where he worked until Joseph E. Brown finally took control of the line. As a black man employed as a mechanic on a Georgia railroad, Thompson was not unique, although in Atlanta, where blacks generally held only semiskilled and unskilled positions, he was certainly atypical. Diverse journeymen performed all but the simplest repairs on the engines. The nature of the particular job determined whether they worked as a group on the shop floor or labored independently with the assistance of subordinate workers.[14]

In the car shops, specialized handicrafts dominated the production process, the rolling stock customarily being constructed mostly of wood. For painting and carpentry, the railroad companies generally drew on local population. Accordingly, eleven of forty carpenters on Atlanta railroads before the war resumed their old positions in the postbellum era. Carpenters and painters, like journeymen in the motive division, exercised considerable job control in spite of managerial supervision of the overall production process.[15]

A variety of semiskilled wage earners augmented the work force in the car shops. Greasers, linters, low-ranking painters, and washers worked on cars in an intricate division of labor under the direction of skilled workers and supervisors. Blacks comprised only a few of the local semiskilled shopworkers, enumerated variously between six and ten in 1870 and thirteen in 1880.[16]

Journeymen's helpers rounded out the labor force in the department. Through extrapolation, local source materials suggest the broad outlines of tasks helpers in Atlanta's W&A shops performed. That employees designated as helpers usually appeared on the 1865 payroll immediately following the names of one or more skilled workers (generally blacksmiths and boilermakers), and that occasional references to "blacksmiths and their helpers" appear in management correspondence, suggest the likelihood that helpers answered directly to individual journeymen.

During January 1865, for example, W&A blacksmiths John M. Spann, J. L. Griffin, J. E. Lee, and W. C. Dorsey supervised a crew of helpers, including Peter Weeks, James Darnald, C. T. Hancock, and J. R. Peters. The appearance of these helpers on company payrolls distinguished the railroad shops from the iron mill. While in iron manufacturing, helpers

received compensation directly from the craftworkers who had subcon-
tracted for their services, helpers in the railroad machinery department
remained employees of the companies. That in February 1865, Weeks,
Darnald, and Peters worked under boilermaker J. F. Garmaney cor-
roborates this generalization; for the helpers were not bound to serve particular skilled workers exclusively, even as they functioned in close
association with one another in their respective assignments. Significantly, their daily wages, which in 1865 stood consistently at $6.70, re-
mained considerably higher than the $5 per day paid to semiskilled
locomotive firemen, though markedly lower than the $7.50 many car-
penters in the car shops received. Unquestionably, then, helpers played
a vital role in the work process in the railroad shops, rendering them more
than mere dispensable laborers.[17]

Until approximately 1880 it was the road departments of the various
railroad companies across the nation that engaged the largest percentage
of laborers, amounting to at least one-third of the industry's workforce.
While the total number of blacks and their ratio to whites remain indeterminate and varied by locale, nevertheless, blacks certainly formed only
a small proportion of these workers.[18] Typically, workgangs performed
the tasks in the road department. Teams building and maintaining
bridges incorporated semiskilled and unskilled workers, as well as skilled
carpenters and painters. These employees worked under gang supervisors, who, in turn, reported to a hierarchy of superiors. Meanwhile, section gangs, comprised of four or more hands and a supervisor, repaired
tracks. Assigned to designated sections of the lines, these laborers tightened spikes, replaced ties, and leveled ballast. The integrated skills utilized in the road department and the interdependency required of all
employees in performing tasks assured that in most cases relations at the
workplace between the section supervisor and the other members of the
section gangs must have been personal, particularly when the supervisor worked alongside the section hands.[19]

Grooming the margins of the roadways, distributing ballast, and in the
rare event of blizzards, shovelling snow from the tracks, gangs of "maintenance of way" workers kept the lines open. Typically, railroads subcon-
tracted these laborers from local employers with large crews. Given the
employment picture in Atlanta, with its abundance of black casual
workers, many of these day laborers probably were black. Their relation
to the various grades of regular railroad company employees was merely
incidental.[20]

Task differentiation and gradation of workers characterized operations in the transportation department. This work process subdivided into two spheres: the locomotive and the caboose. A rigid hierarchy of command and intensive job specialization molded work in each setting. The work group operating a locomotive consisted of an unskilled woodpasser situated at the rear of the engine, who fed fuel from the wood or coal tender to the semiskilled fireman, positioned at the left front of the cab. He stoked the fire, heating the boiler to generate steam powering the engine. By regulating the flow of steam, the skilled engineer controlled the movement and speed of the engine. The engineer's skills also extended to performing routine maintenance on the locomotives.[21] Yard and switching service differed in that semiskilled hostlers and their helpers (being engineer and fireman trainees, respectively) maneuvered engines around the terminals to disassemble and build the freight and passenger trains engineers drove.[22] Among hostlers and their helpers, work dynamics paralleled those of engineers and firemen.

By its nature, the railroad conductor's work evolved differently from that of the locomotive crew. While engineers and their subordinates mastered the mechanics of engines, conductors scarcely needed such technical knowledge. By the post-Civil War period, the ideal conductor functioned as a business agent. Predictably, then, passenger-train conductors ranked superior to freight conductors. In all cases, however, conductors monitored the people and freight in passage. To that end, the conductor implemented schedules, supervised the brakemen and train-hands (who loaded and unloaded freight on all trains), and enforced rules on all in-service train operations, including those of the engineers. (During the 1850s, railroad company managements generally withdrew the authority for conductors to collect fares, leaving that task to ticket agents.) Attempting to distinguish themselves from fellow workers, conductors cultivated distinct manners and modes of dress. At the same time, they endeavored to extract deference from co-workers based on power they wielded over train operations.[23]

Between conductors and brakemen—their apprentices, at least in theory—relations typically proved not so congenial as those linking railroad engineers and firemen, even as, particularly in the North, promotion customarily followed from brakeman to trainhand, then to freight conductor, and ultimately to passenger conductor. That locally brakemen remained so isolated from their superiors as to be excluded from the conductors' union, even as junior partners, relates both to features defining the two occupations generally and to factors peculiar to Atlanta, as a

Southern railroading center. Whereas workers operating the locomotive had sustained interaction, the work routines of conductors and brakemen mediated against shared experiences. Brakemen, who defied death running along the tops of moving cars to apply the brakes (the Westinghouse brake which was perfected in 1869 only gradually being put into service), and who continually risked injury coupling and uncoupling cars before the adoption of the automatic coupler, shared little in common with conductors. Significantly, these distinctions carried over into spheres beyond the shop floor, as well, brakemen generally living and socializing away from their superiors—the conductors—in keeping with their characteristic bachelor status and low income.[24]

The particularities of Southern railroading also influenced interactions between Atlanta conductors and brakemen. So long as slaves and later freedpeople worked as brakemen throughout the region, that occupation bore the stigma of low status. Moreover, the hiring of slaves for the job early on prompted management to alter the standard advancement pattern from brakeman to conductor. A few conductors on Atlanta's railroads around 1860 had commenced their careers as trainhands; but matriculation was so slow that most lower-order railroad workers left the community before attaining such advancement. Especially in the years following the war—an era of expanding political patronage— appointment to the conductor position, in fact, resulted less often because management recognized an individual's experience on the job than because of the individual worker's personal contacts and political affiliations.[25]

Structurally, this division of labor pervading all spheres of the railroad industry set the boundaries of interactions at the workplace across skill lines. While several hundred Atlantans worked in the railroad industry during the Reconstruction years, characterizing how they interacted as individuals at the workplace proves elusive.

## 4. Social relations on the job

Relations which individual skilled railroad workers developed with their employers, as opposed to those they established with fellow wage earners, received most attention by contemporaries. Journalistic tributes paid to Joel C. Kelsey, are illustrative. After the war, Kelsey, a white machinist on the Georgia Railroad, could boast of an exemplary work record in the car shop. Furthermore, on the occasion of Kelsey's death in 1872, one obituary characterized the deceased as "very popular with all classes." Over several years, Kelsey's civic involvements were wide-ranging. Besides belonging to the Mechanics' Union, he was also a member of the city's Mechanics' Fire Company, No. 2, and presumably had affiliated with the Presbyterian Church, where his widely attended funeral was held. Of import, as well, in 1847, Kelsey had joined with his workplace supervisor, William Rushton, the socially prominent master-mechanic of the Georgia Railroad, in organizing the Atlanta Masonic Lodge, No. 59. In this connection, Kelsey socialized intimately with such business and professional personalities as A. C. Ladd, a prosperous coal and lime dealer, and E. J. Roach, a leading physician.[26] Apparently then, as his personal connections and organizational affiliations indicate, Kelsey participated in the bourgeois society around him, likely aspiring to achieve middle-class status himself. How he interacted with other shop-workers, both skilled and less skilled, the reporters evidently concluded, warranted no attention.

In most cases, however, even in the absence of overt class conflict, workers formed bonds of friendship and mutuality with workmates rather than with employers. Cumulatively those relations arose in large measure out of particular work situations in which members of primary work groups came to share common perceptions of their collective interests. As Atlanta newspapers touted entrepreneurial capitalism, the characteristics of working-class life, which news reporters ignored and editors rejected as unnewsworthy, typically passed unexamined. In retrospect, then, they remain shadowy.

Such socialization always had the potential of evolving in any of several directions, as influenced by the economic, social, and political dimensions of the world outside the workplace. On the job, the wage earners' common employment, their shared attitudes about employers, and their similar prospects in life created a condition conducive to the nurturance of working-class consciousness. Other factors, however, exerted a countervailing influence. Successive operational cutbacks in the railway industry, after the Civil War and during the depression of 1870s, took a toll on the workers employed by the W&A, in particular. Nationwide economic crisis and their own employment insecurity heightened the alienation employees experienced, often pitting them against each other on such issues as layoffs and the consequent increased workloads management imposed on survivors.

One W&A wage earner told a *Daily Herald* reporter in 1872 that "the wages now paid were barely sufficient to support the wives and children of the men respectably; that the work to be done was more severe than before . . . because the force had been greatly reduced." Pressed by the reporter as to why, under the circumstances, the employees did not initiate a job action to redress their grievances, the wage earner averred that under company policy, strikers were to be replaced summarily by compliant strikebreakers.[27]

Management's implementation of arbitrary policies on such issues as employee safety, as well as favoritism in the delegation of work assignments, invariably sparked conflict in labor-management relations. By consistently placing certain workers in advantaged positions over others, though, the railroad management diminished the potential for workers to organize an effective opposition. All the while, ongoing racial tension in Atlanta allowed management to threaten malcontent employees of low rank—who were least likely to benefit from promotion to supervisorial positions—with replacement by eager recruits if they defied management prerogatives.[28]

Using corporate paternalism, as manifested in company picnics, the W&A management cultivated the allegiance of strategic groups of white workers. While, in staging these periodic rites, W&A officials wooed white employees "from the superintendents down to the track raisers," they uniformly excluded black workers. In response, on at least one occasion, the black wage earners organized a separate outing.[29]

In the social relations among railroad employees, the degree to which workers internalized the values implicit in the concept of racial determinism shaped their individual and collective interactions. Accordingly, the structural dimensions of the workplace influenced the outcome by providing a context for confirmation or refutation of those assumptions. Operating on this principle, the W&A management sought to influence the process in its own interests.

Railroad employment of Atlanta blacks, approximately 77 to 90 in 1870 and 133 in 1880, was highly stratified on the basis of color. Throughout the period, no black held the post of engineer and none achieved the rank of conductor. In 1870, five worked as hostlers, this number increasing to 24 in 1880. A few blacks were firemen in 1870, but their numbers diminished subsequently, concurrent with changes in locomotive technology that eased the job and attracted more whites into that line. Nor did blacks fare better over time as brakemen, the numbers dropping from 7 or 8 in 1870 to 4 in 1880. With improved brakes, the work of brakemen became safer, prompting whites to seek those jobs as well. Most blacks remained in the unskilled ranks of the machinery, road, and transportation departments, despite the fact that they were regular employees.

Compounding these limitations on the black employees' opportunities, management implemented cost-cutting measures by laying off blacks before whites, while extending general preference to whites over blacks in new hiring.[30]

Even though blacks were a minority of railroad employees and had few prospects for promotion out of the lower ranks, white workers feared competition by blacks. That after the war, whites and blacks worked together on railroads, of course, had precedent. Throughout the antebellum period, slaves had labored on lines across the South. Some had even worked as brakemen, engineers, station hands, and shop mechanics, in which capacities they interacted with white workers. Because slaves had established themselves in all roles of railroad work elsewhere throughout the South—even if not so much in Atlanta itself—after the war, white railroad employees felt anxious about the possible impact on their jobs of a mass infusion of blacks into the industry. Events seemed to support their anxiety. When several black Atlantans petitioned the United States Army authorities during 1867, demanding additional employment of former slaves on the W&A—at a time when many white railroad workers were jobless and underemployed—pressure mounted. Moreover, white workers remained concerned that employers would arbitrarily replace dissident whites with allegedly compliant black workers. When management instituted lower pay for black employees than for whites in the same work, the fears of the latter group of wage earners gained ever greater credibility. While employers repeatedly had extended hiring preference to higher-paid whites, the institution of racially based wage differentials within job classifications effectively undermined the potential for white workers to pressure their employers for additional economic concessions.[31]

At the same time, while whites were hostile to the blacks seeking railroad work, tension did not build on one side alone. Black train workers and those who merely hoped for such employment had their own grounds to protest the whites' domination of the industry by virtue of their color. When they did obtain railroad employment, the blacks consistently were extended no opportunity to advance out of the lowest-level positions. This structural inequality emerged early as a source of contention. By petitioning the United States Army in 1867, Austin Wright and the nine co-signators protested against industrywide discrimination, particularly in appointments to entry-level positions of trainhands, depot workers, and baggage masters. Being consistently the last hired and lowest paid—but the first dismissed in periods of labor-force retrenchment, despite their individual job tenure and mastery of skills—sowed seeds of discontent among the black workers.[32]

Distrust which developed among and between Atlanta's white and black railroad workers, therefore, initially arose in large measure out of manipulative workplace policies managers adopted to control their workers by exploiting the racially charged postwar environment. When white wage earners internalized those values, benefiting in limited measure (at least in the short run) from those discriminatory practices in the work process, tension surrounding the social relations of production mounted. The resulting division among workers—along craft, skill, and racial lines—effectively pitted them against one another.

These dynamics prevailing, the cases when Atlanta railroad employees even partially bridged the differences among themselves proved exceptional. In one notable instance, several car-shop mechanics joined with other groups of skilled workers from across the city to promote their common interests in the political arena. In 1869, these craftworkers cooperated in the organization of Workingmen's Union, No. 1, which briefly heightened popular interest in local electoral politics.[33] Generally, however, the workers proved too divided among themselves to respond effectively as a unified body to management on wage and job-control issues. Examination of the sequence of Reconstruction-era railroad strikes involving Atlantans illustrates the contradictions.

Conflict first erupted in February 1871, when the W&A announced a new policy designed to free the company from financial obligation to the workers and their survivors in job-related accidents. Henceforth, according to a management directive, as a condition of employment, all employees were to sign "death warrants" absolving the company of any accident liability. Citing the injustice of this policy, substantial numbers of the black workers united in a strike action, walking off their jobs. The railroad's business did not suffer long, however, for whites readily signed the documents and replaced the striking black workers, thereby legitimating the oppressive management policies.[34]

In August 1872, when confronted with yet another round of wage cuts, W&A mechanics contemplated job actions to force management to hold wages at prevailing levels. All planning ended abruptly, however, after the company announced it would replace dissidents with other railroad workers.[35] Having earlier divided along craft, skill, and racial lines, the workers found themselves unable to mount a united opposition.

In November 1876, craft divisions pitted the conductors on the Georgia Railroad against its engineers. When the Brotherhood of Locomotive Engineers struck against management's proposed thirty-percent wage cut for engineers, even non-unionist engineers spontaneously supported the work stoppage. Firemen and hostlers quickly joined the protest, as well, though newspaper reports did not indicate whether black workers joined the white strikers.[36] Yet, while engineers, hostlers, and firemen showed solidarity, the conductors—also union men—guarded the idled trains as company property in their charge. Standing with the company to protect the trains from sabotage, the conductors lent credence to threats that by hiring strikebreakers, or scabs, management would soon have the locomotives running again.[37]

Just one year later, in 1877—the year of the Great Upheaval—when firemen on the W&A belonging to the Brotherhood of Locomotive Firemen threatened to strike over wage issues, engineers informed the company that, as a group, they would not join forces with their defiant subordinates. "They are determined to stick to the road," the *Atlanta Constitution* reported about the engineers, "and will not sympathize with any discontent or effort on the part of anybody to interfere with the trains." Against the backdrop that year of crippling railroad strikes spreading across the nation—covered extensively in the local press under such provocative headlines as, "A Riot in Louisville, Flavored With A Touch of Communism"—this pledge of local engineers holds particular significance.[38]

Under fire on their jobs, then, Atlanta's skilled railroad workers saw promise in the prospect of organizing conservatively along craft lines, following the emerging national pattern. Such collectivity would enhance their prospects in negotiating with management on basic wage issues. Also, the union would provide fellowship with co-workers, and mutual aid benefits to alleviate the burdens of this dangerous occupation.

## 5. Railroad workers and craft unionism

Following craft lines, engineers, firemen, and conductors across the United States organized national unions during the 1860s and 1870s. In 1888, machinists set up the National Association of Machinists, with Atlanta as the first local. Only beginning in the 1880s did semiskilled employees, such as maintenance-of-way workers and railroad brakemen, form unions.[39]

Among railroad employees, locomotive engineers were the first to organize a national union, the Brotherhood of Locomotive Engineers (BLE), in 1855. This body formally convened for the first time in Detroit during 1864; delegates adopted a constitution incorporating firemen and machinists, as well as engineers, into the organization. At the second BLE convention, however, participants amended the constitution, excluding all but locomotive engineers.[40] Thus, when, in January 1867, activists organized Local No. 69 in Atlanta, the BLE operated on a craft basis.

From its inception, the BLE sought to achieve orthodox trade-union aims through conventional tactics. Continually union president Charles Wilson emphasized the transcendent commonality of interests among employers and union leaders. "A number of railroad officials" with whom he had acquaintance, Wilson told BLE conventioneers in 1867, "have heretofore been prejudiced against the Brotherhood, but I am happy to inform you that they are now its warmest advocates and friends." In his view, education of both workers and management about the principles of trade unionism promised to mitigate conflicts in management-labor relations. Accordingly, he prophesied, "no conflict can possibly arise in regard to wages or [work] rules, if the parties can be made to believe that their principles are mutual.[41]

Proceedings of the 1874 annual meeting of the national union in Atlanta reaffirmed values Wilson had enunciated in 1867. "We come here," one speaker assured residents of the host city, as well as the assembled delegates, "with no mischievous doctrines or purposes, and seek no interference in anything beyond our proper sphere, although [as] a labor organization and the employees of railroad companies we recognize the mutual interest which makes a company's success and its employees['] welfare a common cause. At the same time," he continued, "we claim no right to dictate or interfere in the affairs of any company, nor ask anything but the common rights of the laborer who is worthy of his hire. The policy of our association is protective and co-operative, but never aggressive."[42]

Within these parameters, the programmatic objectives of the engineers' union addressed matters on two planes. First, the union advocated contractual guarantees for the eight-hour day and improved (or at least stabilized) wages, despite the general retrenchment. At the same time, especially under the influence of union president Wilson, the BLE emphasized charity and self-improvement, particularly through fostering temperance and implementing of an insurance and benefit system.[43]

In pursuit of those goals, the union advocated conciliatory relations with employers, despite the sustained assaults railroad companies nationwide had launched on train workers, including the members of the BLE. Specifically, the BLE advocated the imposition of formal arbitration and bureaucratic procedures to negotiate and administer contracts between the workers and management. To reinforce the union's ideological and tactical conservatism, delegates ratifying the BLE constitution approved a ban on "political discussion" in all proceedings, even in the routine affairs of the locals, as well as all forms of official union participation in electoral politics. Accordingly, the national leadership categorically rejected alliances with the National Labor Union, the Knights of Labor, and socialists.[44]

Only occasionally did grumblings of discontent indicate rank-and-file dissent from official union goals, strategies, and tactics. An unsigned article in the *Locomotive Engineers' Monthly Journal* is illustrative. The author did not question the legitimacy of the abstract hierarchical relation between capital and labor. But he did attack "the insatiable greed" molding the capitalists' attitudes about workers, whom employers considered as subject to their absolute control. "There is not a capitalist in the whole country," the article proclaimed, "who is not cudgeling his brains to conjure up some new device by which he can reduce the laborer, already battling with want and hunger, to the very verge of starvation, anxious to try the experiment whether a man is not capable of doing the same amount of work though hungry, if he has sufficient food to barely sustain life." The worker's power, the author reminded readers, was rightfully the property of the wage earner. Workers and capital, he contended, should exchange the products of labor amicably on the basis of mutual respect. Despairing of that prospect, the contributor concluded with a plea for the organization of all segments of labor so that no capitalist could again attack a worker without confronting the wrath of the whole working class.[45] Calls for working class unity, such as this one, seldom appeared in the engineers' journal, and there is no indication that the Atlanta local was any less conservative.

Similar dynamics characterized other railroad unions with Atlanta membership. During the 1870s, Georgia's locomotive firemen had set up a society to provide insurance and to act on wage issues. Ousted from the BLE in 1865, firemen across the country organized their own national craft union, the Brotherhood of Locomotive Firemen (BLF). By 1877, Georgia firemen, including those in Atlanta, appeared to have been active members.[46] Stressing civic responsibility and harmony in social relations as supreme virtues, the BLF consistently precluded itself from serving in any direct role as a catalyst of class consciousness. "The Brotherhood of Locomotive Firemen," the young Eugene Victor Debs, then editor of the *Firemen's Magazine*, wrote in 1885, "has taught, from its inception to the present time, and shall continue to teach . . . the identity of the interests of capital and labor, believing that all their business relations conducted with this fact in view, will be harmonious and friendly, and avoid what might otherwise result in discord and strife." To that end, Debs concluded, BLF members should endeavor to meet their employers on fair terms, a position which earlier had induced Debs to condemn the railroad strike of 1877 as incendiary.[47] Consistent with this vision, the BLF adopted as its primary function the provision of sickness, injury, and funeral benefits. Also, the union lobbied with railroads nationwide to standardize promotional procedures, to assure that management recruited locomotive engineers from the ranks of the firemen.[48]

Meanwhile, in 1874, conductors on the several Atlanta lines affiliated as Division 22 of the Brotherhood of Railway Conductors (BRC), in 1879 renamed the Order of Railway Conductors. The aims of this national union included temperance reform and the provision of mutual aid and insurance to members.[49] In the aftermath of the 1877 national railway strike, moreover, the national union leaders furthered their conservative vision by implementing a rule prohibiting union members from striking.

By opposing strikes, the BRC leaders shared a common stance with BLE and BLF officials. The conductors carried their no-strike law to such an extreme as to arouse opposition within their own ranks, prompting the union to rescind the law in 1890. Nevertheless, the message reiterated in Atlanta at the November 1875 BRC national convention, and again at the Railroad Conductors' Life Insurance Association convention in the same city in October 1877 (enthusiastically reported in the *Atlanta Constitution*) apparently influenced Atlanta railroad workers. As we have seen, in 1876, Georgia Railroad conductors intervened on behalf of management against their fellow workers when they guarded company property against striking engineers and firemen. This, and similar actions nationwide, motivated some members of other train workers unions around the country to criticize the BRC for weakening all the other unions in the industry.[50]

While skilled railroad workers sought to build strong trade unions, the narrowness of their strategies and tactics stunted their growth into the

1880s and beyond. Organizing along craft lines, skilled railroad workers institutionalized arbitrary distinctions among themselves which limited their effectiveness in confronting their common employers. Moreover, their elitism compromised their strategic options by precluding an inclusive organization representing all workers within the industry. By nurturing exclusionary tendencies, these craft unions isolated members, cutting them off from wider working-class support which otherwise might have transformed communities. As a result, these craft organizations remained weak throughout the Reconstruction era.

In effect, gains these higher-rank railroad workers achieved through their trade unions depended on their ability to monopolize the technical knowledge embodied in their skills. As this strategic concern converged with ideological assumptions widely diffused in postwar Atlanta culture concerning the natural hierarchy of racial types, the form of labor organization in which these workers engaged embodied all the contradictions implicit in those visions. In the postwar setting, then, the characteristics of Atlanta's racially split labor market (like that of the rest of the South) determined that railroad craft-union organizers had two substantive strategic choices. Either they could incorporate blacks into the previously all-white organizations as equals, or they would have to drive all blacks out of the craft jurisdiction, assuring that only whites would advance into the elite ranks, and that white and black workers would not fraternize. Without hesitation, nationally, the BLE, the BLF, and the BRC pursued the latter course, in the process drawing only nominal dissent from some Northern members. This outcome is not surprising. The pervasiveness of cultural values upholding white supremacy, the dynamics of social interaction in the community, and the complex pattern of production relations at the workplace which railroad managers so methodically had institutionalized in hiring and promotional practices—all reciprocally reinforced that racial segregation.[51] Without a trade union base, then, black railroad workers had to develop alternative means to promote their collective interests. Like those who, in 1871, protested against the W&A management's policy on occupationally related injuries, aggrieved blacks sometimes engaged in wildcat strikes. Others, outside the industry but hoping to be hired by the W&A, addressed petitions to government officials requesting employment.[52] Both in petitioning and striking, blacks often perceived no alternative to portraying their interests as distinct from—if not opposed to—those of white workers. The impact of institutionalized divisiveness only reconfirmed those hostile visions members of each group had developed about the other in a self-reinforcing syndrome.

Divided as they were along craft, skill, and racial lines, then, the men employed on Atlanta's railroads could hardly generate experiences of collectivity that might point toward challenging the status quo imposed by the railroad managers. In the vacuum, lower-rank railroad workers were unable to sustain any organization, while the unionized skilled workers nurtured a narrow vision of community, one bereft of any inclusive solidarity among wage earners. Unwilling to repel sustained management initiatives against them with a unified resistance embracing all employees, the BLE struggled merely to subsist through the depression of the 1870s. In an 1867 letter to the union journal, Local 69 member J. B. Travis reported that Atlanta's local represented some 35 engineers. By January 1875, when P. M. Arthur, national president of the BLE, visited the city, the local boasted 60 members, a circumstance which induced him to characterize its condition as "flourishing." Business records of the Atlanta local, however, challenged the accuracy of Arthur's description. Indeed, during 1875 and 1876, several issues of the union journal reported numerous expulsions of members from the Atlanta local for non-payment of dues. Apparently as early as 1875, then, members were encountering economic difficulties. Communications from Local 69 in the journal thereafter appeared with less regularity. Even the routine listing of the Atlanta local as an active affiliate became sporadic during the winter of 1878, disappearing altogether by October 1879.[53] In 1881, a Minnesota local assumed the designation Local 69.

In Atlanta, the BLF had an equally unstable existence during the 1870s and 1880s. Unable to count on even the engineers to support them in actions such as their 1877 W&A work stoppage, the firemen could sustain little more than a skeletal organization throughout the Reconstruction era. A letter in an 1885 issue of the union journal described firemen in Atlanta as ripe for organizing, suggesting the local there had folded.[54]

Briefly, between 1885 and 1887, some segments of Atlanta railroad workers adopted a different tack in organization. In those years, Local Assembly 4335 of the Knights of Labor attempted to bring together workers at various trades into a single body.[55] Following the collapse of Knights nationally, this Atlanta local assembly dissolved in 1887. In its wake, skilled railroad workers remained unorganized, reflective of their fractionalized past. Ultimately, in 1888, carshop machinists of Atlanta were to launch the National Association of Machinists, while engineers, firemen, and conductors would reorganize into more militant job-conscious trade unions, although these were still grounded on craft distinctions and racial divisiveness during the 1890s.[56]

Thus the dilemma of Atlanta's railroad workers—rooted in their divisiveness along craft and racial lines—remained unresolved. The skilled workers withdrew into narrowly based and racially exclusive craft unions, while the unskilled, who also were unorganized, found themselves fragmented and without collective strength to promote their own interests.

## The Rolling Mill

### 1. Scope of operations

The largest manufacturing enterprise in postbellum Atlanta—the Atlanta Rolling Mill—was the city's other principal employer.[57] Of course, by comparison with the nation's largest rail factory—the Cambria Iron Works of Pennsylvania, with 40,000 acres of mineral land, dozens of furnaces, a Bessemer converter, and an 1872 payroll of 6,000 men and boys—operations in Atlanta were on a small scale. Yet even by national standards, the Atlanta plant—with its rolling mill proper, a foundry, and a nail factory—was not insignificant.[58] Moreover, its activities affected the livelihoods of a major portion of Atlanta's labor force. In the immediate aftermath of the war, with demand high for tracks to rebuild the damaged lines around Atlanta, prospects for the resurrected Atlanta Rolling Mill looked bright, a prognosis which local workers doubtless welcomed.

### 2. The labor force

The number of rolling mill employees—all males—fluctuated over time according to the mill's production capacity and the shifting demand for iron products, which reflected national economic conditions. Describing the plant in 1870 and 1871, writers variously recorded employment there as 320 and 250. A nationwide glut of iron rails—among the Atlanta mill's leading products—dampened local iron manufacture during 1871. Two years later in 1873, with the onset of an industrial depression, the ranks of Atlanta Rolling Mill workers dwindled to 200. By mid-1875, employment edged back up to between 300 and 400, despite the mill's serious cash-flow problems. Then, in 1879, when the economy rallied and

*The Atlanta Rolling Mills, Marietta Street.*
From E.Y. Clarke, *Atlanta Illustrated, Atlanta*

iron output surged, as many as 500 Atlantans were on the company payroll. Their jobs at the mill, however, were short-lived. A crippling strike in 1881, derivative of and compounding the company's long-standing financial woes, prompted management to lock out the workers. Before the issues in contention were resolved, fire destroyed the plant.[59]

## 3. Skill division and race

In general terms, mill workers were divided into three categories: unskilled, semiskilled, and skilled. Precise figures on the proportion of the total force each of these component groups represented are not available. Even in the Northeast, where compilation of statistics on workers and industrial production for the period tend to be the most complete, numbers for iron and steel manufacturing firms do not provide a consistently clear picture. Fragmentary information indicates that through 1876, the comparatively primitive rolling mill technology required a high proportion of skilled workers, having physical stamina and metallurgical knowledge, to work with the metal. Strong unskilled laborers, in some plants comprising twenty percent of the workforce, also were indispensable.[60] Over the next ten years, innovations in the organization of production, including improved product flow and the subdivision and integration of tasks in the work process, altered the industry. Even as the organization of work changed, the introduction of labor-saving equipment transformed the work process. The development and implementation of hydraulic hammers and shears, of cranes and automatic conveyer tables in rolling mills, and, after 1866, the adoption of the Bessemer converter and the "basic open-hearth steel process" that standardized chemical processes gradually reoriented the industry toward higher-grade iron and steel production. Evidence indicates that the cumulative effects of these innovations lowered the demand for skilled workers and increased the proportion of semiskilled machine tenders in the mills. The evidence for the impact of these changes on the demand for laborers is less clear.[61]

Because fire destroyed the Atlanta Rolling Mill in 1881, iron manufacturing locally did not undergo the organizational and technological alterations characterizing Northeastern plants from 1881 through 1886. Even before 1881, however, the management's persistent financial difficulties, coupled with depression and the local abundance of cheap, nonunionized labor, apparently weakened the incentive mill managers might otherwise have felt to change the work routine by improving the methods of pig-iron production and by altering the composition of the labor force. Compared to operations in Pennsylvania, or to mills in Richmond, Virginia, and Birmingham, Alabama—all close to sources of raw materials—the Atlanta Rolling Mill functioned at a relative economic disadvantage.[62] Thus, the proportion of low-skilled laborers in the Atlanta Rolling Mill between 1876 and 1881 did not expand as rapidly as in other mills, where changes in work process and technological innovations promoting specialization and intensive division of labor undercut craftworkers.

In Atlanta, skilled workers—puddlers, rollers, and molders—were preeminent in the occupational hierarchy. One May 1875 account mentioned sixteen puddlers in the mill's employ. Just how many rollers and molders worked at the plant over time remains unknown.[63] In the traditional craft-manufacturing mode of iron production, skilled workers hired "helpers" independently. These helpers, not to be confused with unskilled laborers and apprentices, worked directly under the journeymen's supervision in production tasks. Iron and steel puddlers typically hired one or two helpers each, while rollers hired twelve on the average.[64] Extant source materials on the Atlanta Rolling Mill do not indicate precisely the numbers of such employees, though the mill labor force probably included about thirty puddlers' helpers and a large number of rollers' helpers.[65]

Distinctions among iron-mill workers by race reinforced skill stratification, as management routinely discriminated by color in hiring and promotion practices. In Atlanta, white mill workers apparently concurred in this policy, for it yielded at least short-term benefits in their own employment. Over time, whites monopolized the skilled positions and dominated most semiskilled jobs. Even Irish and German immigrants who entered the mill as menial laborers could anticipate rising into better remunerated and more secure semiskilled and skilled jobs. Such prospects did not extend to blacks, who, in 1870, comprised more than twenty percent of the mill's work force. During Reconstruction, black males found jobs at the rolling mill in the lowest paid stratum of laborers. With few exceptions, most blacks received no promotions for the duration of their careers.

Through the force of circumstances, however, a small proportion of these blacks mastered operations requisite to semiskilled and occasionally even skilled jobs. Thomas Albert was one such exception. At age twenty-nine, Albert commanded sufficient skills to feel confident in identifying himself to the 1880 census enumerator as a rolling mill molder. Probably he worked under the supervision of white journeymen. Yet the success Albert and others of similar accomplishment enjoyed, albeit limited, alarmed white workers determined to protect what they considered their own sphere of employment. Consequently, white craft-workers institutionalized these relations by excluding blacks from the Atlanta locals of the Iron Molders' Union (IMU) and the Amalgamated Association of Iron and Steel Workers (the Amalgamated).[66]

### 4. Wages and race

Racial stratification in rolling mill occupations had a corollary in the employees' wage differentials. Predictably, the instability of the era undermined the economic status of all employees—blacks and whites. By the end of the Civil War, skilled workers' representatives routinely negotiated with management on a particular rate per ton for the finished product based on a sliding-scale system. This standard pegged journeymen's (and consequently their subordinate helpers') wages to the market price of iron. As self-contained production units under the direction of the various craftworkers actually conducted mill operations, the journeymen haggled separately with their helpers and apprentices over wages they would receive from the earnings of the craftworkers.[67]

The disparities of this system were readily apparent in that rollers, molders, and puddlers retained four to five times what they paid their helpers. Such earning power afforded the craftworkers options to purchase material amenities enhancing their domestic lives. At the same time it eliminated the economic imperative for all members of their families to work—at least until the crisis of the 1870s took its toll.[68] Helpers and laborers, meanwhile, could not afford bourgeois accouterments.

With the mill management sustaining racial distinctions in wage policies, the situation for the one in five mill workers who were black, most of them concentrated at the low-skill end of the employment hierarchy, remained particularly bleak. Working for a dollar per day, black laborers reportedly earned only one-third of the wage paid whites for similar work. This differential spurred management to make some cuts in overall labor costs by replacing certain higher-priced white laborers with cheaper black hands. The effect was job losses even for whites. Here, then, were dark sides of what historian David Montgomery has characterized otherwise in more favorable terms as "workers control."[69]

Moreover, in their lack of employment security, the black workers were particularly vulnerable to financial crises when the national economy fluctuated drastically. The slump in the iron industry during the 1870s created serious hardship for white mill workers, with periodic reductions in wages and hours of employment. For blacks in the industry, however, the turn of events proved devastating. Unskilled as most of them were, they lacked the collective strength and strategic control over their own labor power which would have assured them bargaining clout. In the end, employers, including rolling mill managers and journeymen in all departments, viewed individual black workers as dispensable. Such conditions prevailing, blacks laboring in the Atlanta Rolling Mill, as in mills elsewhere in the South, had few alternatives but to accept the low wages proffered them by employers when, indeed, there was any work to be had.[70]

## 5. Skill definition and division of labor

Though the labor force was atomized, mill operations functionally integrated the workers, thereby summoning the coordinated effort of all personnel, from unskilled to skilled. Schematically, iron manufacturing activated chemical processes at controlled temperatures to transform ore into altered form.[71] At the Atlanta Rolling Mill, employees performed these steps in two departments: one the mill building proper, and the other a foundry and nail factory. Combined, eleven furnaces facilitated operations, six of them being in the foundry. Other machinery included two squeezers and one puncher. Power derived from eight engines, which, in turn, ran on steam from eleven boilers.[72] Continuous-process iron production, then, required the coordination of many hands.

This work process gave rise to extensive division of labor along craft lines. At the same time, the interdependency of these tasks assured that workers of all skill levels—organized as formal work groups—contributed to the end product. Iron rolling, for example, required the coordinated labor of rolling teams comprised of skilled rollers and a variety of helpers. The process commenced when the rollers and management settled on a lump sum to be paid to the rolling team per ton produced. Once the figure was decided, rolling team members conferred and divided the pay variously among themselves according to their individual skills. At the same time, they agreed on task assignments and determined the number of rounds on the rolls they would make each day. Utilizing raw materials provided by the management, the employees then commenced work, exerting themselves in stints of intense labor punctuated by periods of rest. The heaters drew upon considerable technical knowledge in conducting the firing process, while unskilled roughers, catchers, and hookers pressed the hot iron through trains of grooved rolls to produce up to sixty tons daily of iron rail, as well as bars, plates, and nails, all of which the mill sold.[73]

Casting wrought iron in the foundry involved different operations conducted by similar work groups. Routinely, the puddler fired the furnaces at three or four in the morning to melt the ore for rabbling, a process of stirring the hot iron in the furnace, exposing it to oxygen, and skimming out impurities. Learning job-related chemistry and cultivating the ability to judge temperature changes in metal were among the accomplishments of this skilled worker. Once the iron had been rabbled, the molder took command, working with the assistance of helpers. "Eyeballing it" and using intricate handwork, the craftworker "rammed" and "poured" the molten iron into forms yielding wrought iron objects. When, alternatively, the molders filled orders for merchant bars, or made castings for railroad-car wheels, mill gearing, and iron fronts and verandas for buildings, they pounded the refined metal into the required shape, using iron-headed hammers weighing several hundred pounds each.

Martha and Murray Zimilies have captured some of the dimensions of the molders' physically taxing work. "Men wielded heavy tools such as iron tongs six feet in length to carry bars of iron, often weighing over one hundred and fifty pounds." All the while, "sparks flew and hammers swung, often burning and maiming." Furthermore, the buildings in which these activities centered "were poorly ventilated, and during the summer became infernally hot. Men often collapsed, muscles were torn, and lungs were ruined from smoke and gases." Given these conditions, it is not surprising that the workers labored with the molten ore in forty-minute stints, after which journeymen and helpers took rest periods. Usually the molders remained in the vicinity of their workplace during the breaks. Puddlers and their helpers, however, customarily adjourned to nearby beer halls where they fortified themselves for the next round of stiflingly hot and dangerous work.

Significantly, puddling and molding, unlike iron rolling, remained immune to mechanization until late in the nineteenth century. Thus, the craftwork mode of production, with its considerable autonomy, persisted in the case of puddlers and molders, while deskilling transformed the rollers' work process, even at the Atlanta Rolling Mill.[74]

Conducting this continuous-process work, journeymen depended on helpers whose services they contracted individually. Given the variety of activities in the mill, helpers performed tasks ranging in character from those of low skill (catchers and roughers) to precision work (heaters). Each of these steps, in turn, was interrelated to subsequent tasks, and therefore required a team effort.[75]

There was the general observance of these skill delineations and of the division of the labor among journeymen rollers, puddlers, and molders, on the one hand, and their helpers, on the other. Nevertheless, across the nation, conflict among these workers was ongoing. Friction surfaced periodically when the journeymen attempted to recoup from the helpers (as their own employees) the losses they had themselves sustained when the mill management, plagued by a depression economy, imposed wage cuts against the rollers, puddlers, and molders, while demanding higher productivity. Compounding this problem, journeymen faced skill dilution and overcrowding of the labor market when mill owners took the offensive to enhance their own power by rationalizing the production process, thereby undermining the craftworkers' traditions. In response, individual journeymen felt their only short-term remedy was to cut their helpers' wages, if not to replace the helpers altogether with less experienced, but lower-paid "green hands," while they also reaffirmed the exclusionary practices of craft unionism. In the long run, such practices only further undercut the journeymen's position. An influx of low-wage laborers commanding even limited practical training could always easily be manipulated into strikebreaking.

For the helpers, the issue in contention remained that of the exploitative practices of the journeymen with regard to wages and working conditions. While such tensions apparently did not lead to job actions in Atlanta, helpers in some mills elsewhere in the country did resist attacks on their wage rates. Using their vital roles in the production process to their own advantage, they launched strikes against their journeymen-employers, and sometimes sided with management in strikes by the craftworkers. That such outbreaks did not materialize in Atlanta itself does not indicate an abatement of those conflicts in that city. Indeed, Atlanta's own besieged iron workers likely followed those episodes, as reported in newspapers and the union press.

Ultimately this industrywide conflict was not resolved until the mid-1880s and later—several years after fire destroyed the Atlanta Rolling Mill. At that time, journeymen of the Amalgamated, under attack by iron manufacturers across the land and responding to the organizational successes of the rival Knights of Labor, would commit themselves to

broadening the base of their union by organizing metal workers along industrial lines, including all wage earners throughout the mill. This development extended protection to the helpers for the first time.
Furthermore, by codifying in union rules limitations on the use of
helpers, the Amalgamated asserted the primacy of the collective interest
over the journeymen's self-serving goals.[76]

Work done by iron mill laborers was less precisely defined. Some were
hired for maintenance and custodial duties and to stoke furnaces. After
the Civil War, moreover, Southern iron masters recruited blacks as pig-
iron carriers and loaders. In these latter positions, teams of laborers syn-
chronized with the pace skilled workers set. Such a work process, with
its pre-industrial character, was familiar to the communally oriented
former slaves, inducing many of them to seek out such work situations.[77]
While blacks comprised a substantial portion of the unskilled laborers at
the Atlanta Rolling Mill during the Reconstruction period, native-born
and immigrant whites also worked in that capacity, though little can be
determined about the interactions of these groups.[78]

## 6. Craft unions and workers'-control struggles

Following the war, Atlanta's middle class generally interpreted the
gifts and fetes some workers periodically gave their supervisors and employers as portending harmonious labor-management relations. Indeed,
such expressions of loyalty and dutifulness as rolling mill workers showed
their superintendent P. A. Smith in presenting him "a magnificent gold
hunting watch" manifested the close interpersonal relations of
nineteenth-century iron manufacture, a dynamic which often assumed
a paternalistic form.[79] These rituals, however, revealed but one aspect of
a complex relationship.

Controversy over the role of craft unions in the rolling mill and
workers'-control struggles further shaped social relations among the rolling mill workers. In the 1870s and into the early 1880s, the Atlanta Rolling Mill emerged as one site of the conflict that rocked the
iron-manufacturing industry across the South, when skilled white workers
defended their prerogatives on the contested terrain of the shop floor.

Skilled workers—being the elites in the craft system of iron
manufacturing—early demonstrated responsiveness to unionization.
When William Sylvis, as president of both the IMU and the National
Labor Union, visited Atlanta in 1869 on an organizing drive through the
South, he reported meeting with "first class men" to discuss union prin-

ciples and to reestablish a local of the molders' union. Those he encountered already had some familiarity with the IMU. A local had existed in the city previously, but was suspended because of the members' allegedly faulty understanding of the union's objectives and "dull times." Changed circumstances prevailing in Atlanta on the occasion of his visit inspired Sylvis with high hopes for the new local.[80] Still, the local did not flourish, even though the molders initially had expressed interest.

Beginning in the 1870s, iron barons across the nation took the offensive against their employees, denouncing the IMU and the Amalgamated for conspiring to socialize the mills, which they insisted were their private property. Rhetoric notwithstanding, the conflict setting workers and iron manufacturers at odds centered on personnel policies, company business practices, union recognition, and the operatives' determination to control the labor process through the preservation of self-managing production teams on the shop floor. In the judgment of mill managers, workers' power could be contained only when the mill owners rationalized the production processes, by taking the technical knowledge out of the hands of the hitherto indispensable craftworkers.[81]

From the 1860s onward, these iron-worker trade unionists had contended with their employers on wages, the posting of rates per unit on the piece-rate system, and the method of disbursement. In May 1875, a crisis in labor-management relations forced the issue to a head in Atlanta, as well as nationally. Mill employees in Atlanta desperately awaited payment of $11,000 in back wages due them for several months of work. Not only had the company defaulted on wage payments, but, in providing subsistence to keep the workforce operational, the management instituted a "company store" policy. Thereby, employees were directed to make their purchases at the company-owned store, the medium of exchange being credit against the wages they had coming, set at 60 to 65 cents on the dollar owed them, a policy they generally rejected. Then, mill manager Lewis Schofield's decision to fire three puddlers who were union activists, raising the issue of employment security for union members, prompted molders and puddlers to initiate a strike that other mill workers promptly joined. In response, Schofield raised the stakes by ordering workers "to sign an agreement, that among other things, [they] should not act together as a union in any matter whatever pertaining to the mill." Reconciliation that followed was short-lived. Only weeks later, as the same grievances persisted, mill workers launched a second job action that lasted at least two days. Not long thereafter, the financially strapped mill went into receivership. The subsequent group of employers had better business success, turning a profit of some $50,000 in their first year administering the mill.[82] However, economic uncertainty in the industry nationwide, exacerbating the instability of the Atlanta Rolling Mill operations, left its employees with unstable jobs for the duration of the depression.

Similar issues surfaced again in 1878 when, once again, the financially insolvent mill management fell into arrears four months on wages and disputed with employees over an acceptable form of payment. In late March, workers walked out of the plant, striking for more than one week. Conflict on this occasion reminded at least some of the molders of the advantages they might derive from resurrecting their defunct union. In early April 1878, the IMU revived the charter for Local No. 153.[83]

Perceiving the threat unionization represented, the mill management denied the IMU recognition as the molders' bargaining agent. A second walkout followed in May 1878, in the course of which workers demanded that the court having jurisdiction over the bankrupt mill appoint a new management. In the aftermath, Grant Wilkins became the court-designated receiver. Significantly, these early strike actions had the support of a sufficient number of employees to halt plant operations completely.

Under the authority of the new receiver, mill officials fought back during 1879 by reinstating "iron clad agreements," which the iron molders had resisted effectively since 1875. Known also as "yellow dog contracts," such legally enforceable restrictions on employment compelled workers to acknowledge that their hiring was contingent on not belonging to a union and on pledging abstinence from work-related organizational activities for the duration of employment.[84] "Iron clad agreements" obviously posed a problem for the molders of Local 153. Yet, these craftworkers were not alone in their discontent, for across the country, skilled iron workers watched with alarm as their employers concertedly undermined craft-union organizing efforts.[85] When conditions at the Atlanta Rolling Mill deteriorated further during May 1881, roughers, heaters, and rollers joined in common cause against an intransigent management to form Atlanta Lodge No. 1 of Georgia, of the Amalgamated Association of Iron and Steel Workers.[86]

For these higher-rank iron workers, it should be noted, the battles did not revolve solely around wages, business practices, and formal union recognition. In the fast-changing industry, they were determined to preserve their discretionary powers in making unilateral decisions on work-process matters and they sought to incorporate these prerogatives in union work rules at local and national levels. At the same time, the craftworkers attached importance to job-security issues. Once hired, the workers insisted, they had a perpetual right to their jobs, unless charges of incompetence, negligence, drunkenness, or laziness could be sustained against them. Even though other issues were more prominent in the Atlanta Rolling Mill strikes of May 1875 and July 1881, the workers also saw the principle of job security at stake. Persistent management attempts to weed out union activists kept the issue alive in Atlanta as throughout the nation. Union members also continuously had to fight for strict enforcement of seniority in promotions.[87] Thus, the iron workers regularly invoked the concept of fair play to justify their positions.

Still, for skilled iron workers, the most significant control struggles centered on preserving their customary power to set production levels for the furnaces and roll tables. As the industry had evolved, heaters and rollers routinely had set the number of "heats" and "rounds" which they deemed to comprise an honest day's shift, while puddlers and molders had stipulated the weight or size of the metal charges they would feed into the furnaces and the appropriate number of "pourings" of molten metal to be made daily. For their part, iron puddlers had set standards on the grade of iron ore supplied to them. Less-costly low-quality ore, the puddlers maintained, did not heat well; and they refused to work under conditions forcing undue physical exertion. Once unions formed in the individual mills, workers customarily had codified these practices in union work rules. Thus, by regulating the pace of production and maintaining a standard pay scale, skilled workers had denied their employers a guaranteed profit margin they would otherwise have achieved through wage cutting and layoffs, as the fluctuating economy dictated. Their accustomed power, the craftworkers maintained, assured their health and physical capacity for work.[88]

That they could control production stemmed from the historical bonds among craftworkers which were continuously regenerated. The demands they imposed on the iron manufacturers, then, far from being revolutionary, were based on their own practical experiences in their respective crafts and were shaped by their determination to preserve their prerogatives threatened by change.[89]

Even though production depended as much on the craftworkers' skill and experience as on their aggregate technical knowledge about chemical processes, the skilled workers' determination to protect their positions rankled the efficiency-minded, profit-oriented mill owners, who intended to alter the balance of power. "Irresponsible committees have dictated terms and laid down rules to which masters have had to conform," charged an irate writer in the *Iron Age* of January 1878. "They have decided the market price of labor, have said who should or who should not be employed or restricted the privilege of employers to do what they will with their own." To curb such practices and transform the production process, iron manufacturers concluded that their own interests necessitated asserting control in the workshops to change basic operational patterns.[90]

The main thrust of the managers' program to curb iron craftworkers' autonomy involved reorganizing the work process by intensification of the division of labor to dilute the skills required of individual operatives. At the same time, the managers endeavored to impose authority from the top down in all mill operations. Such policies, iron manufacturers believed, would check the skilled workers' strategic advantages in job control. Furthermore, through such measures, the mill operators sought to destroy the iron craftworkers' collective self-definition, the unity which had helped them sustain their power.[91]

Circumstances peculiar to Atlanta, as noted above, limited the potential for iron production in the city. Economics and logistics weighed most heavily in undercutting the momentum for rapid expansion of the Atlanta Rolling Mill. At the same time, the low wage rate, assured by the large surplus of black and white workers at all skill levels, minimized management's incentive to defeat the union through deskilling the work process. Therefore, operations at the local rolling mill were not subject to the high degree of mechanization characteristic of plants elsewhere in the nation.

Once the IMU and the Amalgamated had organized sufficiently to wield power over operations at the Atlanta plant, however, the management, under receiver Grant Wilkins, stepped up its offensive to destroy the unions. Thus, in July 1881, management triggered a lengthy strike when Wilkins fired Lem Poss, a puddler and Amalgamated member, replacing him with William Smith, presumably not a unionist. As the strike dragged on into August, Wilkins resorted to the proven tactic of exacerbating racial tensions among the workers by hiring more than 200 blacks to recommence production. Among the blacks brought in as strikebreakers, those who were skilled were likely hired at a lower wage than the white union members whom they replaced. Then, Wilkins obtained a court injunction restraining those participating in the job action and their union strike committee "from in any manner 'interfering' with the working of the mill or influencing the men in any shape or form." In the final strike settlement, Wilkins announced a company policy that the mill workforce was to be comprised of forty percent black and sixty percent white employees. This policy would have doubled the percentage of blacks at the mill and marked the first opportunity for them to work regularly in skilled positions, presumably as puddlers and molders.[92]

By pursuing this course to change the dynamics of production, management indirectly exposed the contradictions and limitations in the white skilled iron workers' concepts of mutuality and community. At the same time, the managerial strategy played on the distrust blacks felt for the white workers in light of the racial exclusiveness of the craft unions. With mounting tension, the potential for an emergent working class alliance across racial lines languished.

Industrywide, over time, this alteration of the social relations of production and the work process transformed the production of iron from the traditional "manufacturing" mode to that of "modern industry."[93] Because a fire of undetermined origin gutted the Atlanta Rolling Mill immediately after the strike settlement, the plant did not survive long enough for implementation of the intended transformations.[94] Nevertheless, the settlement suggests the direction of management policy.

## 7. Social relations at the point of production

These aspects of work at the rolling mill, then, influenced the social relations among workers at the point of production. Reinforcing the effect of established work routines, the close quarters of the plant—the rolling mill was 350 by 180 feet and the foundry 50 by 100 feet—assured that employees constantly interacted with each other.[95]

Within this context, the interplay of ethnicity and race warrants consideration. Numerous studies of postbellum working-class communities in the Northeast assess ethnicity as a variable influencing occupational experiences.[96] In Atlanta, however, ethnicity did not adversely affect rolling mill employees. Along with native-born whites, immigrants held jobs in all occupational classifications in lesser or greater proportion. Furthermore, both groups interacted continuously on the shop floor, which circumstance, in some cases, profoundly influenced their lives.

In the mid-1870s, Thomas Fitzgibbon, John Kelly, and Pat Wakely— all Irish expatriates—were rollers at the Atlanta Rolling Mill. Their experiences corroborate these assertions about the role of ethnicity at the workplace. Turning out iron, they labored alongside both native-born Americans and other newcomers, including James Smith, a white New Jersey native employed as a roller, and Michael Wise, a German immigrant working as a heater. Their common circumstances as higher-rank rolling mill personnel seemingly overcame any latent ethnic exclusivism, for these several men carried over their shop-floor acquaintance to their private lives. All roomed together in the home of William Ferry, a rolling mill supervisor, and Matilda Ferry, his wife.[97]

Evaluation of this group of rolling mill workers points to essential dynamics of interpersonal relations. Where immigrants worked as "green hand" helpers at the iron works, they functioned in a problematic relationship to other more experienced helpers and to journeymen who hired them. Yet not all the immigrants were helpers, nor were all helpers foreign-born. Therefore, among Atlanta iron workers at least, it would seem that no polarization along immigrant and native-born lines in employment opportunities prevailed. Furthermore, there is no evidence that rolling mill managers segregated workers along ethnic lines to any significant degree. Seemingly, the relatively small size of the immigrant population, as well as war damage to Atlanta and the popular sentiment to rebuild the city so as to regenerate the local economy, militated against ethnic conflict in the workplace. Consequently, there was little development of ethnic divisiveness that might otherwise have polarized Atlanta wage earners. White native-born workers could not easily isolate and discriminate against immigrants, for the delineation of their position in society was not so absolute as the color line.

While relationships between native-born whites and European immigrants in the Atlanta Rolling Mill generally remained benign, those between blacks and whites (both native and foreign-born) tended to be of a different character. The roots of this underlying racial tension among the mill employees arose out of the antebellum heritage of social relations.

Recently some historians have begun to reappraise the roles of slaves and white wage earners in Southern industry, including iron manufacturing, from the late eighteenth century through the Civil War. Surveying antebellum Southern manufacturing, Fred Siegel argued that the region's employers remained competitive with Northern interests solely by controlling a cost-effective slave labor force, which they employed alongside an elite corps of skilled whites. The incentive to switch slaves from agriculture into manufacturing increased in proportion to the declining price structure in antebellum Georgia agriculture during the 1840s and early 1850s, and again in the late 1850s.

Employment patterns in Virginia iron manufacturing from the late-eighteenth century through the Civil War sustain this hypothesis. Ronald L. Lewis has argued that, during these years, slaves comprised a steadily increasing proportion of the Chesapeake-area iron industry workforce. Initially, slaves labored under the control of planter-industrialists, and, from the 1840s, in the command of entrepreneurial industrialists. According to Charles Dew, slaves at the Oxford Iron Works in Campbell County, Virginia, from 1812 to 1813, engaged in all stages of production. Dew found, furthermore, that the molder supervising the foundry was also a slave. At this factory, gender formed no basis for distinction in task assignments, as slave women performed some of the most strenuous tasks at the blast furnace and on the ore banks, digging and raking as well as cleaning the ore. Lewis noted, additionally, that when the Confederacy conscripted whites, blacks took control of production, even assuming skilled roles which whites had monopolized previously.

Not surprisingly, therefore, most white workers in the Southern manufacturing sector viewed slave labor in the factories as reducing their own bargaining power on wages and working conditions, for structurally the lower-paid, captive black labor force provided employers a wedge with which to undermine resistance by white workers. Increasing reliance on slave labor in industrial production, indeed, sometimes in skilled positions, heightened this anxiety. White wage earners became convinced that even those positions which, by virtue of their race, had previously been guaranteed to them, were no longer secure.

To eliminate this competition by slave laborers, white workers campaigned in several Southern cities for passage of suitably targeted minimum-wage laws and taxation laws, as well as for outright restrictions on the employment of slaves in various occupations. The opposition of entrepreneurs who dominated the political power of those cities, however, consistently defeated such initiatives, except in Georgia. There, legislators enacted laws in 1845, 1849, and 1850; but enforcement lagged, due to employer resistance.[98] Inevitably, these developments in the Southern economy informed the perspectives of white iron workers about black wage earners and their employers following the war, as well.

As industrialists slowly established footholds in the Southern economy and retooled their factories, white workers who sought employment in Atlanta's plants recalled the considerable inroads blacks previously had made into the industrial labor force across the South, particularly during the war years. Subsequently, their worst fears seemed to be confirmed. Not only did blacks attain jobs as iron mill laborers, but in some instances, they circuitously worked their way even into skilled positions, from which vantage point they competed with white craftworkers. On this matter, a superintendent of the Atlanta Rolling Mill related to Sir George Campbell during the latter's visit in 1878, "that there are instances here of negroes developing much mechanical skill and conducting themselves very well."[99] Skilled white iron workers viewed this state of affairs as threatening their job security and wages, even when whites supervised blacks.

While white iron workers harbored resentment and hostility toward black employees, the blacks regarded their fellow white workers with perspectives tempered by their memories of slavery and by the social relations of the Reconstruction era. In speculating on the attitudes with which blacks viewed white immigrants, one might assume that rancor prevailed. Writing of changes over time in black attitudes toward European immigrants in Southern society, however, historian David Hellwig argued that in the postbellum period, blacks generally did not view white immigrants as a distinct threat. Because the newcomers settling in the South were comparatively few in number, blacks as a rule did not fear displacement from employment because of the influx of this new white group. Moreover, Hellwig maintained, blacks often expressed compassion for the immigrants, who symbolized the efforts of all oppressed people to improve their positions in the world. Some blacks even hoped the arrival of Europeans would infuse the region with new vitality and direction, while loosening the slaveholders' grip on the land and economy. Blacks in postbellum Atlanta did not record their attitudes about the arrival of foreign-born people in their city. But since they recognized that the major barrier to fulfillment of their own aspirations remained the intransigent white planter society, Hellwig's argument for ambiguity in black perspectives on European-born newcomers probably applied in Atlanta.[100]

However blacks viewed immigrant wage earners, their attitudes about whites generally in Southern iron mills reflected their own defensiveness in the face of unrelenting white hostility. Though blacks recognized that the mill owners' policies on employment, wage differentials, and division of labor exacerbated racial tensions among iron workers, they also perceived that their own interests were damaged by the practices followed by white mill workers. Confronting technological breakthroughs in steel manufacture, besieged white skilled iron workers predictably sought to protect their tenuous positions against incursions by non-unionized, low-wage labor. But, when these same craftworkers internalized the racism of the planters and New South industrialists and attached responsibility to black workers for industrywide economic crises, blacks saw themselves as scapegoats. After all, in Atlanta, they generally held only the lowest-rank jobs, for which they received substantially lower wages than whites. Nor did whites in these trades demonstrate any willingness to pressure their craft unions to repeal constitutional bans on black membership and to organize and promote the interests of black workers in common cause.[101]

Rebuffed by exclusionary trade union policies, some blacks endeavored to acquire production skills on their own, despite formidable obstacles, enabling a small percentage of them to advance beyond unskilled and semiskilled labor. Circumstances not of their own making, then, induced black iron workers to undercut the union wage scale, which tactic sometimes yielded them mill jobs. While white mill workers viewed such practices as evidence of the blacks' irresponsibility, these same blacks held the recalcitrance of the white unionists as confirmation of white hostility. The outcome of the conflict proved disastrous. When, ultimately in 1896, long after the Atlanta Rolling Mill fire, the IMU expediently changed its policy, officially seeking to enlist both black and white workers, black molders generally refrained from affiliating with what they deemed a hostile institution.[102]

With respect to the iron mill workers, both black and white, the element absent from Atlanta after the Civil War—a factor which might otherwise have altered or even redirected the goals and tactics of the wage earners—was an alternate experience providing them a vision of an inclusive working-class collectivity. Had such an ideal for Atlanta seemed viable, iron workers conceivably might have identified their mutual interests irrespective of socially defined racial differences and organized interracial coalitions to confront common problems at the workplace and in their community. Such coalitions, in fact, did appear, briefly at least, in other Southern cities.[103] But there was none in Atlanta.

In the vacuum, black and white iron workers struggled against one another. Technological changes and alterations in the organization of work in the industry opened some new employment prospects to black laborers. In response, whites tightened their hold on skilled jobs.[104] The context of distrust and conflict among black and white workers thus persisted and seemed to be reconfirmed by events industrywide, including in Atlanta.

Notably, national union records substantiate that, between the end of the Civil War and 1879, there were few instances of blacks breaking white iron-workers' strikes. Yet, these isolated cases so indelibly impressed white trade unionists as to abort coalitions of black and white iron workers.[105]

In the minds of white wage earners at Atlanta's rolling mill, events surrounding the protracted 1881 strike by skilled white workers validated these judgments about the alleged strike breaking proclivities of black workers. The evidence seemed incontrovertible that blacks had cooperated with management by resuming the plant's operations, thus undermining the unions' strength.

Despite management's move, striking iron workers attempted to sustain their morale as evidenced in one striker's correspondence to the *National Labor Tribune*, the official journal of the Amalgamated:

> There is no change here in regard to the mill from last week, only this: they have succeeded in starting the puddle mill. All of them are darkeys, and are doing well, so they and their trainers say; but I don't know. . . . The boys are still solid and happy. Last Saturday was our pay-day. We received our benefits . . . from the National Lodge, and we also received fifty dollars from Chattanooga lodge.

Yet frustration about the situation in light of the employment of the black workers crept into the communication when the writer conceded that, "some of our brothers are leaving here."[106] Ultimately the strikers lost on this issue of the employment of blacks when the management insisted on allotting sixty percent of the jobs to union members, but mandating forty percent for the strikebreakers, some of whom were holdovers from the prestrike work force.[107] While fire destroyed the mill before the settlement was fully implemented, the outcome of the strike exacerbated the enmity of white iron workers for blacks at the mill. Indeed, as Mary Freifeld has noted, the concepts of an "ethic of the 'white man'" and "the code of 'manliness,'" which union members used with reference to the principle of solidarity in strike actions and support for the union, reflect the racist dimensions which had become incorporated into the culture of white iron workers.[108]

## Foundries

Workplace dynamics in Atlanta's smaller foundries provide an important comparative perspective. During 1871, four or five foundries operated locally. Excluding the Atlanta Rolling Mill, six functioned in the city ten years later.[109]

With twelve to sixteen workers, Herman Franklin's tin-stove factory was the smallest of these establishments.[110] The Joseph Winship & Brother's Foundry and Machine Works of Atlanta operated on a somewhat larger scale. Indeed, prior to the Civil War, the Winship foundry ranked as the city's largest manufacturing plant, with a force of some forty wage earners who manufactured and repaired freight cars. After the wartime destruction, which gutted the foundry, and its subsequent resurrection, operations resumed with a force of thirty in 1871, rising to upwards of sixty-five workers by 1880—all involved in the production of iron railings and grates, iron for cotton gins, and a variety of other agricultural implements.[111]

Just as the labor force of the Atlanta Rolling Mill functioned in a hierarchical framework, so, too, did workers at the Winship foundry. Skilled mechanics in the latter plant earned an average daily wage of $2.75. Laborers earned about a third as much.[112] Evidence about what role, if any, blacks played in the workforce of these smaller enterprises remains thin and circumstantial. A news item in a local newspaper recorded that when a 1,500-pound grindstone burst at the Withers and Jones Foundry, "[none] of the workmen were hurt," though "a negro man was slightly hurt on the hand."[113] This fragment, together with evidence of urban black males generally working as laborers throughout the city, including at the rolling mill, suggests that at least some blacks held similar positions in the smaller foundries.

The small size of these operations and the nature of capital formation at the local level raise the probability that the enterprises were tightly controlled as family ventures. Owners of these small enterprises could not afford to implement potentially explosive employment policies which would have risked disruption of production and might have damaged the fabric of employer-employee relations.[114]

In sharp contrast to the unfolding events at the Atlanta Rolling Mill, relative tranquility prevailed in the smaller foundries. While operations in the larger plant were subject to organizational and technological changes and while management demonstrated its intent to restructure the social relations of production accordingly, such was not the case in the smaller foundries. Examining the iron industry in the late-nineteenth century, David Brody has argued that wrought iron manufacturing—the chief enterprise of these small foundries—was not subject to cost-cutting improvements because of technological constraints.[115] Presumably traditional modes of making wrought iron prevailed in the foundries specializing in such operations. That no local newspaper reported job-control confrontations in the small foundries further suggests the prevalence of a more paternalistic ethos in small plants, which defused expression of overt conflict.

## Summation

In resolving their predicaments, railroad workers in the Gate City and employees of the Atlanta Rolling Mill who joined craft unions opted for an organizational initiative, the internal contradictions of which ultimately constrained them in challenging their employers on the quality of their working lives and on job control. Even though workers of all ranks routinely interacted with each other in complex patterns of social relations at the workplace, the craft unions nevertheless focused their concerns on skilled workers exclusively.

In analyzing the development of the national trade union, Lloyd Ulman asserted that craftworkers resisted inclusion of semiskilled and unskilled workers in their unions on the grounds that the latter two groups inherently commanded little bargaining power, and, at the same time, given the nature of their degradation in the labor market, exhibited an over-eagerness to strike. Were the lower-rank workers to be incorporated into the unions as equal members, the craftworkers feared they would more often be compelled to strike, even when their odds for victory remained low.[116]

Yet, as in the case of railroad and iron mill workers, the outcome of this organizational strategy undercut the potential for the emergence of a collective identity among a majority of railroad and rolling mill employees. By definition, craft exclusiveness structurally isolated the skilled trade unionists from the majority of workers, even when all faced common problems. In effect, craft consciousness dividing workers along skill lines left all sectors of the workforce vulnerable.

Compounding skill distinctions, union proscriptions on black membership exacerbated the workers' divisiveness. As events at the mill demonstrate, policies precluding from membership even those few blacks who had gradually advanced into the ranks of the semiskilled set black and higher-rank white workers at odds with one another. In the wake, white puddlers, molders, and rollers in particular came to fear lower-paid black competitors, while the blacks in the mill distrusted the whites because of their exclusionary policies. Parallels also marked relations among Atlanta's railroad workers. Predictably, at least some of the disillusioned black workers, who long had sought advancement into skilled jobs, resorted to strikebreaking, reinforced by recruits from other cities. At the same time, white workers showed little solidarity with black railroad workers when the latter legitimately struck over intolerable working conditions.

Thus, the overall impact of craft unionism on both black and white Atlanta workers in the railroad and iron manufacturing industries proved problematic. On one level, these skilled workers' unions mounted an intense struggle to protect the rights and workplace traditions of at least a segment of the wage earners threatened by employers' offensives. Yet, on another plane, this organizational form perpetuated fundamental and explosive contradictions within the overall labor force. To the extent that these unions legitimized and reproduced relations based on racial divisiveness and the segmentation of workers by skill, the results impaired possibilities for collectivity in resolving social, economic, and political crises afflicting all workers.

## NOTES

1. Richard Edwards, *Contested Terrain: The Transformation of the Workplace in the Twentieth Century* (New York: Basic Books, 1979), pp. vii–ix, 25–34; Roger Penn, "Skilled Manual Workers in the Labour Process, 1856–1964," in *The Degradation of Work? Skill, Deskilling and the Labour Process*, ed. Stephen Wood (London: Hutchinson, 1982), pp. 105–6.

2. Henson, "Industrial Workers," pp. 184–88; BRFAL, Records of the Assistant Commissioner for the State of Georgia, 1865–69, RG 105, Microfilm 798, Roll 24, Unregistered Letters Received, 7 November 1865.

3. Henson, "Industrial Workers," p. 189.

4. *Atlanta Constitution*, 25 May 1869.

5. Ibid., 3 September 1868, 4 March 1870, 8 April 1870, 4 March 1873; Wynes, "1865–1890," p. 216; Nathans, *Losing the Peace*, p. 103; Henson, "Industrial Workers," pp. 189–91.

6. Stephen Henson uses data on individual workers listed on the W&A payroll to cross reference railroad worker entries on the 1870 census. This method likely explains most of

the variation in numbers of railroad workers for 1870 he and Jerry Thornbery introduce. The latter relies solely on the census. Slight variation may also be due to their differing interpretations of occupational titles. Henson, "Industrial Workers," p. 201; Thornbery, "Development of Black Atlanta," pp. 318–19, 321.

7. Western and Atlantic Railroad Company, Atlanta Division Payroll, January–August 1865, n.p., Western and Atlantic Railroad Collection (hereafter cited as W&A Payroll 1865), Georgia Department of Archives and History, (hereafter cited as GDAH); speech of Col. E. W. Cole to the Georgia Railroad stockholders' convention, *Atlanta Constitution*, 15 May 1875.

8. The observation about the method of payment of the W&A engineers is based on inspection of the 1865 W&A Payroll and subsequent records. Ibid.; David L. Lightner, *Labor on the Illinois Central Railroad, 1852–1900* (New York: Arno Press, 1977), pp. 164–66; George R. Horton and Ellsworth Steele, "The Unity Issue Among Railroad Engineers and Firemen," *Industrial and Labor Relations Review* 10, no. 1 (October 1956): 49–50.

9. Ross M. Robertson, *History of the American Economy* (New York and Burlingame: Harcourt, Brace and World, 1964), pp. 384–85; Ralph Andreano, ed., *The Economic Impact of the American Civil War* (Cambridge, Mass.: Schenkman Publishing Company, 1962), pp. 179–81; (Atlanta) *Daily Herald*, 29 August 1872.

10. W&A Payroll, 1865, n.p.; Atlanta and West Point Railroad Company, Payroll for Division No. 2, October 1865, Georgia Miscellany Collection, Special Collections, Emory University.

11. Henson, "Industrial Workers," pp. 129, 203–4; *Atlanta Constitution*, 10 December 1872, 24 April 1873, 9 June 1874.

12. It should be recalled, as well, that cotton farmers reaped low crop yields from 1865 through 1867. Not only, then, did the railroad industry feel the effects of the seasonal character of agriculture, but the bountifulness of the harvest affected railroad profit margins through its impact on the amount of freightage hauled in any year. Henson, "Industrial Workers," pp. 14–22, 189; *Atlanta Constitution*, 25 May 1869; Western and Atlantic Railroad Company, Superintendent's Records, Outgoing Correspondence, vol. 2 (1868–1870), letter to Joshua Hill, 26 June 1869, Western and Atlantic Railroad Collection, GDAH, (hereafter cited as W&A Superintendent's Records, Outgoing Correspondence); Wynes, "1865–1890," p. 216; Licht, "Nineteenth-Century American Railwaymen," pp. 105–6, 251; Armstead L. Robinson, "Beyond the Realm of Social Consensus: New Meanings of Reconstruction for American History," *Journal of American History* 68, no. 2 (September 1981): 281.

13. Henson, "Industrial Workers," pp. 44–48; Lightner, *Labor on the Illinois Central*, p. 69.

14. Henson, "Industrial Workers," pp. 42–43, 185–87; John H. M. Laslett, *Labor and the Left: A Study of Socialist and Radical Influences in the American Labor Movement, 1881–1924* (New York: Basic Books, 1970), p. 151; Edward R. Carter, *The Black Side: A Partial History of the Business, Religious, and Educational Side of the Negro in Atlanta, Georgia* (Atlanta: n.p., 1894), pp. 71–74; W. E. B. DuBois, ed., *The Negro Artisan* (Atlanta: Atlanta University Press, 1902), p. 17; Lightner, *Labor on the Illinois Central*, pp. 75–76.

15. Henson, "Industrial Workers," pp. 42–43, 185–87.

16. Ibid., pp. 114–15, 127, 201; Thornbery, "Development of Black Atlanta," pp. 319–20.

17. W&A Payroll, 1865, n.p.; W&A Superintendent's Records, Outgoing Correspondence, letter to Milo Pratt, 1 May 1869; Henson, "Industrial Workers," pp. 123–26.

18. Studies relying on the manuscript census for 1870 have yielded widely divergent figures in this regard. Tabulating the number of black track hands in 1870, for example,

Thornbery recorded twenty-four, while Henson, using the same data, tallied only nine. As argued above, furthermore, census enumerators often under-represented the black population, particularly in the case of the working class. Licht, "Nineteenth-Century American Railwaymen," pp. 40–41; Thornbery, "Development of Black Atlanta," p. 319; Henson, "Industrial Workers," p. 201.

19. W&A Superintendent's Records, Outgoing Correspondence, letter to A. L. Harris, 11 November 1869; Lightner, *Labor on the Illinois Central*, pp. 69, 76–77.

20. Lightner, *Labor on the Illinois Central*, pp. 76–77; National Archives Microfilm Publications, Letters Received by the Department of Justice from the State of Georgia, 1871–1884 (Washington, n.d.), Microcopy M996, Roll 3, letter from William S. Montgomery, 22 February 1878; Licht, "Nineteenth-Century American Railwaymen," p. xi.

21. Henson, "Industrial Workers," pp. 77–79, 120–21; Angus Sinclair, *Locomotive Engine Running and Management: A Treatise on Locomotive Engines* (New York: John Wiley and Sons, 1886), pp. 18–23, 39–60; *Atlanta Constitution*, 26 July 1877.

22. Horton and Steele, "The Unity Issue," p. 49.

23. Henson, "Industrial Workers," pp. 91, 121, 191; Licht, "Nineteenth-Century American Railwaymen," pp. 345–46.

24. "Mortality among Brakemen," *Firemen's Magazine* 9, no. 9 (September 1885): 527; Licht, "Nineteenth-Century American Railwaymen," pp. 346–47; Henson, "Industrial Workers," p. 129; *Atlanta Constitution*, 10 December 1872; Alfred D. Chandler, Jr., *The Visible Hand: The Managerial Revolution in American Business* (Cambridge and London: Belknap Press of Harvard University Press, 1977), p. 130; Garrett, *Atlanta and Environs*, 1:865.

25. Henson, "Industrial Workers," pp. 91, 109, 121.

26. (Atlanta) *Daily Herald*, 6 November 1872, 7 November 1872; *Atlanta Constitution*, 6 November 1872, 7 November 1872; Henson, "Industrial Workers," p. 59; *Hanleiter's Atlanta City Directory for 1871* (Atlanta: William R. Hanleiter, 1871), pp. 55, 177; National Archives Microfilm Publications, *Population Schedules of the Ninth Census of the United States, 1870* (Washington, 1965), Microcopy no. 593, Roll 151, Georgia, Fulton County, City of Atlanta, p. 242, (hereafter cited as *Population Schedules of the Ninth Census, 1870*).

27. Henson, "Industrial Workers," pp. 202–3; *Atlanta Constitution*, 20 June 1871; (Atlanta) *Daily Herald*, 29 August 1872.

28. *Atlanta Constitution*, 4 February 1871; W&A Superintendent's Records, Outgoing Correspondence, Letter to A. L. Harris, 11 November 1869; Lightner, *Labor on the Illinois Central*, pp. 66–71; Licht, "Nineteenth-Century American Railwaymen," p. i; Edwards, *Contested Terrain*, pp. 33, 54.

29. (Atlanta) *Daily New Era*, 8 May 1868, 4 May 1870, 5 May 1870, 11 May 1870; *Atlanta Constitution*, 4 February 1871.

30. Thornbery, "Development of Black Atlanta," pp. 318, 319, 320; Henson, "Industrial Workers," pp. 195, 201; Hugh B. Hammett, "Labor and Race: The Georgia Railroad Strike of 1909," *Labor History* 16, no. 4 (Fall 1975): 472.

31. Licht, "Nineteenth-Century American Railwaymen," p. 324; Henson, "Industrial Workers," pp. 108–15, 195–97; Hammett, "Labor and Race," pp. 471–72; Howard W. Risher, Jr., *The Negro in the Railroad Industry* (Philadelphia: Industrial Research Unit, Department of Industry, Wharton School of Finance and Commerce, University of Pennsylvania, 1971), p. 164; United States Army Continental Commands, Record Group 393 (hereafter cited as RG 393), Letters Received by the Commander, Department of Georgia, Petition from Austin Wright et al., 17 November 1867, NARA.

32. Licht, "Nineteenth-Century American Railwaymen," p. 324; Hammett, "Labor and Race," pp. 471-72; United States Army Continental Commands, RG 393, Letters Received by the Commander, Department of Georgia, Petition from Austin Wright et al., 17 November 1867; Henson, "Industrial Workers," pp. 195-97; Risher, *Negro in the Railroad Industry*, p. 164.

33. Henson, "Industrial Workers," pp. 207-9; Garrett, *Atlanta and Environs*, 1:817-18; Jonathan Woolard McLeod, "Black and White Workers: Atlanta During Reconstruction" (Ph.D. dissertation, University of California, Los Angeles, 1987), pp. 321-22.

34. *Atlanta Constitution*, 4 February 1871.

35. (Atlanta) *Daily Herald*, 29 August 1872.

36. *Atlanta Constitution*, 16 November 1876, 18 November 1876.

37. Ibid., 18 November 1876.

38. Ibid., 26 July 1877, 29 July 1877.

39. Prior to 1888, some railroad machinists belonged to the Machinists and Blacksmiths' Union, No. 1, Atlanta, a local union. Harry A. Wheeler, "Introduction," in *Railways and Organized Labor*, ed. P. Harvey Middleton (Chicago: Railway Business Association, 1941), p. xi.

40. Henson, "Industrial Workers," p. 206; Horton and Steele, "The Unity Issue," pp. 50-51.

41. *Locomotive Engineers' Monthly Journal* (hereafter cited as *LEMJ*) 1, no. 10 (October 1867): 18-19.

42. *Atlanta Constitution*, 22 October 1874.

43. *LEMJ* 1, no. 1 (January 1867): 13; *LEMJ* 1, no. 2 (February 1867): 6-7; *LEMJ* 1, no. 10 (October 1867): 20; *LEMJ* 5, no. 1 (January 1871): 5-6; *LEMJ* 7, no. 11 (November 1873): 509; *Atlanta Constitution*, 29 October 1874; Licht, "Nineteenth-Century American Railwaymen," p. iii; Reed Cott Richardson, *The Locomotive Engineer, 1863-1963: A Century of Railway Labor Relations* (Ann Arbor: Bureau of Industrial Relations, Graduate School of Business Administration, University of Michigan, 1963), p. 124.

44. *LEMJ* 4, no. 1 (January 1870): 17-18; *LEMJ* 6, no. 9 (September 1872): 411-12; *LEMJ* 7, no. 11 (November 1873): 507; Brotherhood of Locomotive Engineers, *Constitution and By-Laws of the Grand International Division* (Ft. Wayne, Ind.: Jones and Son, 1868), p. 16; Richardson, *Locomotive Engineer*, p. 124; Licht, "Nineteenth-Century American Railwaymen," p. iii; Montgomery, *Beyond Equality*, p. 188.

45. *LEMJ* 11, no. 12 (December 1877): 552-54.

46. United States, Bureau of Labor, *Fifth Annual Report of the Commissioner of Labor, 1889: Railroad Labor* (Washington, 1890), pp. 40-41; Horton and Steele, "The Unity Issue," p. 51; Mercer Griffin Evans, "The History of the Organized Labor Movement in Georgia" (Ph.D. dissertation, University of Chicago, 1929), p. 29; *Atlanta Constitution*, 29 July 1877.

47. Nick Salvatore, "Railroad Workers and the Great Strike of 1877: The View from a Small Midwest City," *Labor History* 21, no. 4 (Fall 1980): 535-36; *Firemen's Magazine* 9, no. 2 (February 1885): 95-96.

48. *Report of the Commissioner of Labor*, pp. 40-41.

49. *Atlanta Constitution*, 8 March 1874; Edwin Clyde Robbins, "Railway Conductors: A Study in Organized Labor" (Ph.D. dissertation, Columbia University, 1914), pp. 12, 15, 20.

50. Robbins, "Railway Conductors," pp. 12, 20, 22; *Atlanta Constitution*, 2 November 1875; 26 October 1877; Evans, "History of Organized Labor," p. 29.

51. Sterling D. Spero and Abram L. Harris, *The Black Worker: The Negro and the Labor Movement* (New York: Atheneum, 1974), pp. 287-88; Herbert R. Northrup, *Organized Labor*

*and the Negro* (New York and London: Harper and Brothers, 1944), p. 50; Risher, *Negro in the Railroad Industry*, p. 36.

52. Henson, "Industrial Workers," pp. 195–97.

53. *LEMJ* 1, no. 7 (July 1867): 11–12; *LEMJ* 9, no. 1 (January 1875): 32; *LEMJ* 9, no. 6 (June 1875): 325; *LEMJ* 10, no. 11 (November 1876): 512; *LEMJ* 12, no. 5 (May 1878): 224.

54. *Firemen's Magazine* 9, no. 3 (March 1885): 160.

55. Jonathan Ezra Garlock, "A Structural Analysis of the Knights of Labor: A Prolegomenon to the History of the Producing Classes" (Ph.D. dissertation, University of Rochester, 1974), pp. 241–46, 263.

56. Henson, "Industrial Workers," p. 211; Evans, "History of Organized Labor," p. 30.

57. As noted above, the rolling mill during the post-Civil War period was also known variously as the Atlanta Mining and Rolling Mill Company (1866), Scofield Rolling Mill (1874–1875), and the Georgia Iron Works (1881). For purposes of the present analysis, the name Atlanta Rolling Mill will be employed throughout.

58. Montgomery, *Beyond Equality*, p. 9; Andrea Graziosi, "Common Laborers, Unskilled Workers: 1880–1915," *Labor History* 22, no. 4 (Fall 1981): 515; Wilson, *Atlanta As It Is*, p. 125.

59. (Atlanta) *Daily Intelligencer*, 3 June 1870; Wilson, *Atlanta As It Is*, p. 125; *Atlanta Constitution*, 20 September 1872, 14 September 1873, 17 June 1875, 18 June 1879, 7 October 1879, 1 April 1880, 5 October 1881; (Atlanta) *Daily New Era*, 7 October 1876; Daniel J. Walkowitz, *Worker City, Company Town*, p. 11.

60. Graziosi, "Common Laborers," p. 515; John Michael Nuwer, "Labor Market Structures in Historical Perspective: A Case Study of Technology and Labor Relations in the United States Iron and Steel Industry, 1860–1940" (Ph.D. dissertation, University of Utah, 1985), pp. 38–44.

61. Walkowitz, *Worker City, Company Town*, p. 155; Gilson Willets, *Workers of the Nation: An Encyclopedia of the Occupations of the American People and a Record of Business, Professional and Industrial Achievement at the Beginning of the Twentieth Century* (New York: P. F. Collier and Son, 1903), pp. 43–48. Drawing on figures compiled by the State of Pennsylvania in 1887, Graziosi determined that the number of laborers increased significantly following changes in the rolling mill work process. In his industrywide study, however, Nuwer argues that mechanization displaced many unskilled mill employees during this same transitional period. Graziosi, "Common Laborers," pp. 515–16; Nuwer, "Labor Market," pp. 44–46, 73–76.

62. Garrett, *Atlanta and Environs*, 1:713; *Atlanta Constitution*, 20 June 1871, 7 January 1881, 10 May 1881; Gutman, "Workers' Search for Power," p. 35; Walkowitz, *Worker City, Company Town*, p. 11; Clark, *History of Manufactures*, 2:293; Warren *The American Steel Industry*, p. 182; Ronald L. Lewis, *Coal, Iron, and Slaves: Industrial Slavery in Maryland and Virginia, 1715–1865* (Westport, Conn.: Greenwood Press, 1979), pp. 19–20.

63. *Atlanta Constitution*, 16 May 1875. The manuscript schedules of the 1880 population census yield no firm figure on the numbers of individuals in these skilled positions. Enumerators most often noted only that a particular individual "works at rolling mill." Occasionally the occupational title "molder" appeared. Because enumerators counted both brick molders and iron molders, though, ambiguity resulted. Therefore, no figure stands forth as a reliable indicator for molders or rollers. Listing only aggregate numbers of employees by age and gender, the Census of Manufactures provides no relevant figures either.

64. Mary Ellen Freifeld, "The Emergence of the American Working Classes: The Roots of Division, 1865–1885" (Ph.D. dissertation, New York University, 1980), p. 168.

65. This figure on puddlers' helpers is approximate, calculatated on the assumption that

each of the 16 puddlers in May 1875 hired one or two helpers. With the high ratio of helpers to rollers, the estimate of the mill having 500 employees in 1879 gains plausibility.

66. Gary Kulik, "Black Workers and Technological Change in the Birmingham Iron Industry, 1881–1975," in *Southern Workers and Their Unions, 1880–1975: Selected Papers, the Second Southern Labor History Conference, 1978,* ed. Merl E. Reed et al. (Westport, Conn.: Greenwood Press, 1981), p. 30; Hopkins, "Patterns of Persistence," pp. 99, 106, 112–14; (Atlanta) *Daily Intelligencer,* 3 June 1870; Wotton, "New City," pp. 219–20; Thornbery, "Development of Black Atlanta," pp. 210–11; National Archives Microfilm Publications, *Population Schedules of the Tenth Census of the United States, 1880* (Washington, n.d.), Microcopy No. T9, Roll 148, Georgia, Fulton County, City of Atlanta, p. 328 (hereafter cited as *Population Schedules of the Tenth Census, 1880*); Frank T. Stockton, *International Molders Union of North America* (Baltimore: Johns Hopkins Press, 1921), p. 59; Spero and Harris, *Black Worker,* pp. 249–51.

67. David Montgomery, *Workers' Control in America: Studies in the History of Work, Technology, and Labor Struggles* (New York: Cambridge University Press, 1979), p. 16; Clark, *History of Manufactures,* 2:227; *National Labor Tribune,* 9 July 1881; Freifeld, "Emergence of the American," p. 168.

68. Walkowitz, *Worker City, Company Town,* p. 251; Freifeld, "Emergence of the American," p. 168.

69. (Atlanta) *Daily Intelligencer,* 3 June 1870; Wotton, "New City," p. 220; Montgomery, *Workers' Control in America.*

70. *Atlanta Constitution,* 20 June 1871, 7 October 1879; Freifeld, "Emergence of the American," pp. 443–44; Stockton, *International Molders Union,* p. 59; Wotton, "New City," pp. 219–20; Spero and Harris, *Black Worker,* pp. 249–51.

71. Freifeld, "Emergence of the American," p. 179.

72. (Atlanta) *Daily Intelligencer,* 3 June 1870; *Atlanta Constitution,* 20 September 1872, 20 April 1873; Wilson, *Atlanta As It Is,* p. 125.

73. Montgomery has documented these operational dynamics of rolling teams at the Columbus Iron Works of Ohio, 1873–1876. Because the routine was thoroughly integrated into the roller's trade, we can assume similar patterns prevailed in Atlanta concurrently. David Montgomery, "Workers' Control of Machine Production in the Nineteenth Century," *Labor History* 17, no. 4 (Fall 1976): 488–91; Freifeld, "Emergence of the American," pp. 168, 171–72, 401–2; John H. Ashworth, *The Helper and American Trade Unions* (Baltimore: Johns Hopkins Press, 1915), pp. 9, 16–24; *Atlanta Constitution,* 14 August 1872, 10 May 1876.

74. Freifeld, "Emergence of the American," pp. 164–94; Walkowitz, *Worker City, Company Town,* pp. 154–55, 251; Jesse S. Robinson, *The Amalgamated Association of Iron, Steel and Tin Workers* (Baltimore: Johns Hopkins Press, 1920), pp. 105–6, 115n; Stockton, *International Molders Union,* pp. 186–88; Lewis, *Coal, Iron, and Slaves,* p. 18; Martha and Murray Zimilies, *Early American Mills* (New York: Clarkson N. Potter, 1973), p. 94; (Atlanta) *Daily New Era,* 3 November 1866.

75. Freifeld, "Emergence of the American," pp. 168–75.

76. Ashworth, *The Helper,* pp. 9, 32; Freifeld, "Emergence of the American," pp. 175, 443–44; Jesse Robinson, *Amalgamated Association,* pp. 133, 135; Montgomery, "Workers' Control of Machine Production," pp. 490–91, 494–95; Montgomery, *Workers' Control in America,* p. 14.

77. Kulik, "Black Workers," pp. 29–30; Graziosi, "Common Laborers," pp. 515, 520–21; Wotton, "New City," pp. 219–20; Stockton, *International Molders Union,* p. 59.

78. See the manuscript schedules of the 1870 and 1880 population censuses for Atlanta and the city directories for the period, which provide information on place of birth, race, and occupation.

79. *Atlanta Constitution*, 8 April 1873.

80. Jonathan Philip Grossman, *William Sylvis, Pioneer of American Labor: A Study of the Labor Movement During the Era of the Civil War* (New York: Octagon Books, 1973), p. 186; Charlotte Todes, *William H. Sylvis and the National Labor Union* (New York: International Publishers, 1942), pp. 103-4; William H. Sylvis, "Letters from the South," in *Life, Speeches, Labors and Essays of William H. Sylvis*, ed. James C. Sylvis (New York: Augustus M. Kelley, 1968), p. 341.

81. Freifeld, "Emergence of the American," p. 212; Ashworth, *The Helper*, pp. 9, 16-23.

82. *Atlanta Constitution*, 16 May 1875, 17 June 1875; Taylor, "From the Ashes," p. 105.

83. *Atlanta Constitution*, 5 April 1878; *Iron Molder's Journal*, 10 April 1878, p. 118; *National Labor Tribune*, 13 April 1878.

84. *Atlanta Constitution*, 21 May 1875, 3 May 1878, 7 May 1878; *National Labor Tribune*, 24 September 1881, p. 2; David Brody, *Steelworkers in America: The Nonunion Era* (New York: Harper Torchbooks, 1960), p. 81.

85. Rather than criticizing the mill owners for being capitalists, these workers typically attacked their employers' personal vices, specifically their tyrannizing the workers. Freifeld, "Emergence of the American," p. 420.

86. *National Labor Tribune*, 25 June 1881, p. 4; *Atlanta Constitution*, 10 May 1881.

87. Clark, *History of Manufactures*, 2:227; Montgomery, *Workers' Control in America*, p. 16; Freifeld, "Emergence of the American," pp. 407-9; *National Labor Tribune*, 9 July 1881; *Atlanta Constitution*, 16 May 1875.

88. Freifeld, "Emergence of the American," pp. 400-404; Walkowitz, *Worker City, Company Town*, p. 251; Jesse Robinson, *Amalgamated Association*, p. 114; Palmer, *A Culture in Conflict*, p. 91.

89. Montgomery, *Workers' Control in America*, pp. 12, 14.

90. Quoted in Freifeld, "Emergence of the American," p. 395.

91. Walkowitz, *Worker City, Company Town*, p. 251; Montgomery, "Workers' Control of Machine Production," pp. 488-89.

92. *National Labor Tribune*, 25 June 1881, 2 July 1881, 9 July 1881, 30 July 1881; Thornbery, "Development of Black Atlanta," pp. 210-11; *Atlanta Constitution*, 6 August 1881; (Atlanta) *Daily Intelligencer*, 3 June 1870; Jaynes, *Branches Without Roots*, pp. 267-69.

93. Freifeld, "Emergence of the American," pp. 164-94.

94. Garrett, *Atlanta and Environs*, 1:813.

95. (Atlanta) *Daily Intelligencer*, 3 June 1870; *Atlanta Constitution*, 20 September 1872; Wilson, *Atlanta As It Is*, p. 215; Ross E. Beynon, *Roll Design and Mill Layout* (Pittsburgh: Association of Iron and Steel Engineers, 1956), pp. 103-23.

96. Walkowitz, *Worker City, Company Town*; Clyde and Sally Griffen, *Natives and Newcomers*; John T. Cumbler, *Working-Class Community in Industrial America: Work, Leisure, and Struggle in Two Industrial Cities, 1880-1930* (Westport, Conn.: Greenwood Press, 1979); Alan Dawley, *Class and Community: The Industrial Revolution in Lynn* (Cambridge: Harvard University Press, 1976).

97. Population Schedules of the Ninth Census, 1870, Roll 151, p. 149; *Beasley's Atlanta City Directory for 1874*, p. 89; *Atlanta Constitution*, 3 February 1874.

98. Fred Siegel, "Artisans and Immigrants in the Politics of Late Antebellum Georgia,"

*Civil War History* 27, no. 3 (September 1981): 223-24, 228, 230; Charles B. Dew, "David Ross and the Oxford Iron Works: A Study of Industrial Slavery in the Early Nineteenth Century South," *William and Mary Quarterly* 31, no. 2 (April 1974): 195, 198-99; Lewis, *Coal, Iron, and Slaves*, pp. 7, 31-35, 80-103; Claudia Dale Goldin, *Urban Slavery in the American South, 1820-1860: A Quantitative History* (Chicago: University of Chicago Press, 1976), pp. 28-33.

99. (Sir) George Campbell, *White and Black: The Outcome of a Visit to the United States* (New York: Negro Universities Press, 1979), pp. 359-60; Stockton, *International Molders Union*, p. 59.

100. David J. Hellwig, "Black Attitudes Toward Immigrant Labor in the South, 1865-1910," *Filson Club History Quarterly* 54, no. 2 (April 1980): 155-56, 166-67.

101. Alexander Saxton, *The Indispensable Enemy: Labor and the Anti-Chinese Movement in California* (Berkeley and Los Angeles: University of California Press, 1971), pp. 23, 44; Lawrence J. Freedman, *The White Savage: Racial Fantasies in the Postbellum South* (Englewood Cliffs, N.J.: Prentice Hall, 1970), pp. 19-36; C. Vann Woodward, *Origins of the New South, 1877-1913* (n.p.: Louisiana State University Press and The Littlefield Fund for Southern History of the University of Texas, 1971), pp. 221-22; Spero and Harris, *Black Worker*, pp. 248-49; Wotton, "New City," p. 220; (Atlanta) *Daily Intelligencer*, 3 June 1870.

102. Stockton, *International Molders Union*, pp. 59-61; Woodward, *Origins of the New South*, pp. 221-22, 228-29; Spero and Harris, *Black Worker*, p. 249; Jesse Robinson, *Amalgamated Association*, p. 47n.

103. In other situations, such circumstances promoted solidarity in relations among workers across racial lines—at least for an historical moment. On miners, see: Herbert G. Gutman, *Work, Culture and Society in Industrializing America: Essays in American Working-Class and Social History* (New York: Vintage Books, 1976), pp. 121-208. On Birmingham, Alabama, industrial workers and New Orleans dock workers, see: Green and Worthman, "Black Workers and Labor Unions in Birmingham, Alabama, 1897-1915," 2:47-69.

104. Graziosi, "Common Laborers," p. 515; Kulik, "Black Workers," pp. 29-30.

105. Freifeld, "Emergence of the American," p. 516.

106. *National Labor Tribune*, 30 July 1881.

107. *Atlanta Constitution*, 6 August 1881.

108. Freifeld, "Emergence of the American," pp. 514-27.

109. Wilson indicated five foundries, excluding those in railroad shops, were in business during 1871. The city directory for that year however, lists only four plus the rolling mill. Wilson, *Atlanta As It Is*, p. 17; *Hanleiter's Atlanta City Directory for 1871*, p. 13; *Sholes' Directory of the City of Atlanta for 1881* (Atlanta: H. H. Dickson, n.d.), p. 114.

110. Hertzberg, *Strangers Within the Gate City*, p. 41; *Hanleiter's Atlanta City Directory for 1870* (Atlanta: William R. Hanleiter, 1870), p. 237.

111. Wotton, "New City," pp. 29, 175; Charles F. Stone, *The Story of Dixisteel: The First Fifty Years, 1901 to 1951* (Atlanta: Atlantic Steel Company, 1951), p. 12; Wilson, *Atlanta As It Is*, pp. 125-26; Tenth Census, Special Schedule of Manufactures.

112. Tenth Census, Special Schedules of Manufactures.

113. (Atlanta) *Daily New Era*, 10 October 1871.

114. The possibility of a converse scenario of harmonious, comradely relations between black and white workers engaged in work together as equals has no foundation in this particular case, at least. Had such social relations prevailed in the context of postbellum Atlanta (or in American society, inclusively), the circumstances would have received extensive (if

derisive and inflammatory) notice in the local, regional, and national presses. In fact, not the least hint of such a state of affairs appears in general circulation or labor newspapers, or in other literary sources uncovered to date.

115. Brody, *Steelworkers in America*, pp. 3, 8.

116. Lloyd Ulman, *The Rise of the National Trade Union: The Development and Significance of Its Structure, Governing Institutions, and Economic Policies* (Cambridge: Harvard University Press, 1955), pp. 211–12.

# CHAPTER III

# MANUFACTURING, FOOD PROCESSING, CONSTRUCTION, AND SERVICE TRADES

Railroads and the Atlanta Rolling Mill were the only large industries in Atlanta. The majority of enterprises—in manufacturing, food processing, construction, and service trades—were much smaller and less hierarchical in structure. Accordingly, more personal social relations typically evolved in these enterprises. At the same time, employers in these industries also expected to maximize their prerogatives by enforcing gender and racial inequality and craft and skill divisions more or less overtly in the workplace. When conflicts involving labor-management relations arose, employees in these diverse smaller industries, like rolling mill and railroad workers, faced formidable internal divisions. Further complicating their position, to many workers, the paternalism which their employers manifested seemed to suggest a commonality of interest between employees and their bosses. Yet, recurrent crises in their dealings with employers over the nature of their jobs often proved a source of disillusionment for the workers. In response, some endeavored to challenge both the structural divisions and the paternalistic ethos.

## Manufacturing

### 1. Lumber, paper, and planing mills

Numerous lumber, paper, and planing mills situated in and around Atlanta turned out products for the local market, thus figuring prominently among the city's manufacturing enterprises. Seemingly the scale

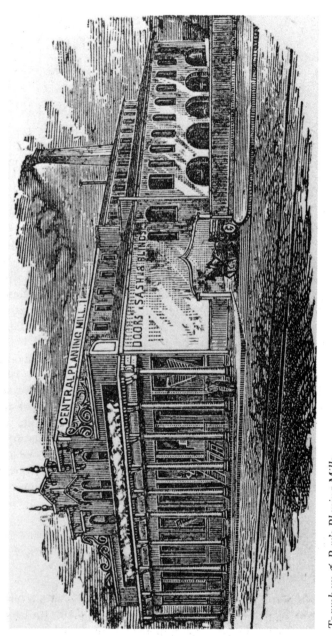

*Traynham & Ray's Planing Mills.*
From E. Y. Clarke, *Atlanta Illustrated, Atlanta*

of these enterprises was not a determinant of their business routines, for some of the larger mills, like many of the smaller ones, operated only part of the year, while others were productive year-round.

The range in the size of their respective labor forces, moreover, reveals further the variations in patterns of mill operations. Most lumber mills were small businesses run by 5 to 10 workers. Thus, W. R. and J. W. Hooper's lumber mill with 20 employees and A. Murphy's with 50 were larger than most similar establishments. Atlanta's two paper mills were among the few such plants in the South. To produce high-quality book paper, William McNaught's Fulton County Paper Mill, (known variously as the Atlanta Paper Mill and the Sugar Creek Paper Mill), retained 33 workers, just under the national average of 35. During the same period, Atlanta's building boom assured the prosperity of local planing mills. Among the four operating in the city in 1870, the Empire Planing Mill employed up to 100 workers. The 1880 census recorded six planing mills, one of which, the Central Planing Mill, regularly had 50 to 75 employees.[1]

In the lumber and paper mills, workers fit into two categories, skilled and unskilled, with corresponding gradations in pay. Across the South, such distinctions correlated with hierarchies of race and gender. Thus, while black males comprised a major group of lumber mill employees, white men uniformly dominated the skilled jobs.[2] During the Civil War, blacks had held at least some of the jobs in Southern paper mills, as evidenced by an extant fragment of a January [?] 1864 payroll for the Fulton Paper Mill listing five black males, probably laborers. No records confirm whether or not blacks held jobs in any capacity at this mill after the war, a period when whites were willing and able to take such jobs, leaving few openings for blacks in Southern paper mills.[3] Assuming the skill distinctions in Atlanta's paper mills followed industrywide patterns, skilled work with heavy machinery remained the exclusive preserve of males. Meanwhile, in sex-segregated crews, white women, who formed almost half of the labor force at the Fulton Paper Mill in 1880, worked in the rag-sorting and shredding rooms, in the cutting rooms where paper was cut to order from large rolls, and in the paper sorting areas where the products were inspected, folded, and separated into lots.[4]

Contemporaries have left no references to unskilled workers in local planing mills, which were less hierarchical and bureaucratic than more "modernized" industries. Seemingly lines dividing skilled workers from entrepreneurs in these plants remained fluid. At the Central Planing Mill, for example, at least one of the three owners, Traynham, had a background as a skilled mechanic and worked regularly in production. Certainly it is worth speculating about the effect of this personalization of management and presumed mutuality of interests between employers and skilled workers in shaping the perspectives of craftworkers. Perhaps, as Herbert Gutman has suggested, the promise held forth by example to skilled workers—that through personal initiative, they shared at least the prospect for individual advancement in occupational rank—checked countervailing tendencies toward working-class collectivism and organized response to their own alienation.[5] Significantly, no reports of collective organization or of "spontaneous" job actions against employers by local planing mill workers appeared in source materials.

## 2. Agricultural implement and carriage manufacturing

A dozen factories in Atlanta manufactured agricultural machinery and carriages after the war. Workers in both these lines used similar skills to turn out products. In fact, the J. J. Ford company engaged in both lines of manufacture from 1865 into the 1870s.[6] On the average, between two- and four dozen individuals worked in these factories, which typically were located in brick tenements. During 1878, however, John M. Smith operated his carriage factory with only 12 employees, while Elias Haiman's Agricultural Implements Company, situated in several buildings spread over three acres, had a payroll of 100 to 150 wage earners. In these plants, a large proportion of the labor force was males over age sixteen, but children also performed some tasks. Whether women and blacks had some of the jobs remains unclear.[7]

Skilled workers in these plants had specialized tasks, including machine fabrication and repair, blacksmithing, wheelmaking, gin building, woodworking, and upholstering.[8] Meanwhile, in keeping the factories operational and in assisting with production, laborers performed diverse functions. Reflecting the two-tiered structure of the labor force, craftworkers on the average received 200 to 250 percent higher wages than their less-skilled co-workers.[9] Such distinctions molded social relations among workers in these enterprises.

The role of entrepreneurs in the production process, as well, seemingly influenced production relations. Shortly after they opened a small workshop in 1869, John M. Smith and David McBride parlayed their fledgling enterprise into a stable business. Experienced in the trades of their own employees, Smith and McBride cultivated personal relations with the workers that suggested a mutuality of interests.[10]

Operations at the Atlanta Agricultural Works, furthermore, seemed to nurture the aspirations of elite skilled workers to become entrepreneurs, therein providing them a clear, if fleeting, incentive to ally with management. While Joseph Johnson owned the mill and its machinery as a capital investment and hired sales agents and bookkeepers, he relegated responsibilities for production, hiring, and wage payment to the six skilled workers who were also department heads responsible for supervising the blacksmith, gin building, woodwork, pattern, and foundry divisions. Each of these individuals was a skilled artisan.[11]

Because locally no episode shattered the surface calm, pitting the workers, as a class, openly against management, how these low-level managers might have cast their allegiances in such a conflict remains unclear. Indeed, as Dan Clawson has argued concerning changes in the nineteenth-century labor process, the position of contractors, both as skilled workers and as low-level management functionaries, was inherently ambiguous.[12] Their backgrounds and assumptions were all firmly rooted in the working class. Yet, circumstances suggest that the convergence of interests between this elite of skilled craftworkers and management potentially promoted a bond between these groups, while driving a wedge into the working class.

### 3. Printing and bookbinding

Printing and bookbinding shops engaged workers with diverse skills. As a hub of the Southeast, by 1870, Atlanta was the home of nine book, job, and newspaper printing firms, of which two—the Franklin Steam Printing House and Bookbindery, and the New Era Publishing Company —also did bookbinding. In bookbinding, these two companies competed with a third, the W. R. Hanleiter Bookbindery. Business expanded rapidly in the ensuing ten years. The 1881 city directory listed fourteen book and job printers and publishers along with several newspaper companies. Bookbinding businesses increased to four.[13] Thus, overall employment in the printing and publishing industry expanded.

Operations of these companies varied in scale. Hanleiter's bookbindery, a small business, maintained a labor force in 1871 of only eight to ten men. Printing firms generally had more extensive plants and engaged more workers. The Atlanta Constitution Publishing Company, for example, had sixty-five on its 1880 payroll, while the Franklin Steam Printing House and Bookbindery hired sixty workers in 1876 and eighty by 1880.[14] Women and children filled varied positions essential to these allied industries, most commonly in semiskilled and unskilled categories. Of its 1880 labor force of sixty-five, for example, the Constitution Publishing Company employed twelve children and three adult females.[15]

Some of the boys who began working in printing at an early age anticipated spending their lives as laborers. Others expected to secure apprenticeships in the industry. Whatever their ambitions, these young laborers worked primarily as "floor boys" and porters responsible for sweeping around and cleaning machinery, and for disposal of scrap lead. Girls characteristically worked to supplement family earnings. At bookbinderies, they most often held unskilled jobs as folders and sewers. Women labored at assembly-line-like work stations in the press rooms and binderies of these establishments. They performed such semiskilled and unskilled tasks as collating, pasting, lettering, folding, and sewing. These jobs were defined by gender, men doing all heavy machine work in separate quarters. Gender barriers that precluded women from skilled positions changed only slowly in the printing trades. Not until 1881 were several women employed as compositors in Atlanta. Gradual mechanization of the press room and book binderies changed the work process, phasing out hand work, such as folding, which girls and women had formerly done. Generally, then, during the postwar era, despite some incremental gains, women's work in the field remained limited.[16]

Adult males formed the majority of the labor force in the printing industry and auxiliary establishments, running presses in the print shops and doing the forwarding and finishing steps in binding, including trimming, rounding, backing, gluing, cutting, sewing, sawing, stamping, and pressing books. Rapid technological change, particularly in printing, of course, deskilled and displaced many workers. Mechanization, though, did not penetrate all branches of the printing trades evenly. Throughout the 1870s, highly skilled and literate men proved indispensable as typesetters.[17]

While age and gender distinctions fragmented these workers, racial categories further stratified employees. Historian David Bennetts observed that approximately six percent of all journalists, printers, pressmen, engravers, copy boys, lithographers, and bookbinders in New Orleans around 1880 were black. Citing racial distinctions in hiring practices in the publishing field, Bennetts attributed even this small presence of blacks in the labor force to employment by black newspapers in the city.[18] Atlanta's blacks, however, did not sustain such a publication in their community. Moreover, whites monopolized the skilled positions on newspapers published in the city. When printers initially formed Atlanta Typographical Union, No. 48 (ATU), in 1860 as an affiliate of the International Typographical Union (ITU), organizers of the antebellum craft union and protective association enrolled white males only.[19]

After the war, fearing that blacks might seek employment with the Republican (Atlanta) *Daily New Era,* thus gaining a foothold in the skilled positions in the printing trades, members of the ATU banned blacks from operating presses under union jurisdiction.[20] Apparently employers complied, as no fight ensued between the union local and the Atlanta publishers. Statements such as one in the *Daily New Era* referring to William Andrews, a black man and former employee of the newspaper's parent publishing company, as "a faithful hand"—in other words, a laborer—suggest, then, the limited range of employment options for blacks in the printing and bookbinding trades.[21]

Stratification of the wage structure reinforced divisions arising from employment patterns. While laborers at the Constitution Publishing Company and at the Franklin Steam Printing Company and Bookbindery earned an average wage of $1 per day in 1880, many women in the bindery shops during 1881 received only $3.50 per week.[22] Nor was the pay for female craftworkers equitable with that for men. Working as compositors, women earned $5 to $10 per week, while their male counterparts on the average received $2.50 per day.[23] One explanation for the disunity within the labor force links discrimination on the basis of gender to the rates of remuneration. A second (or complementary) factor is the possibility that at least some workers in the printing and bookbinding trades found only part-time employment; in any case, organizational and technological changes transforming the industry kept wages low and fostered irregular employment and speed-ups. Simultaneously, while deflation followed the depression of the 1870s, chronic surpluses of workers in these trades, ranging from printers and their helpers down through the ranks of the labor force, yielded competitiveness and tensions, further dividing the work force.[24]

The dilemmas of Atlanta's printing trades workers paralleled those of workers elsewhere in the nation, inducing the ITU to act. When white women or black males sought membership in the union, considerable internal division resulted. After several years of debate during the early 1870s, the ITU adopted a provisional policy on the inclusion of black typographers which extended a local option to union affiliates. Nationally women continued to fight for such a concession into the 1880s. In Atlanta, however, no blacks or women sought to join the ITU, thus sparing the white male membership from any challenge to their union on racial or gender grounds.

From 1865 through 1881, the ITU operated as a stable and mature craft union, notable for its conservative elitism. With eighty active members in the early 1870s, the local pursued traditional trade union activities of mutual aid, and the negotiation and administration of contracts regulating wages and hours.[25] Typographers were the only printing trades workers to sustain an effective trade union. Few conflicts resulted in strikes, assuring that the fraternal aspects of the union attracted most attention among skilled workers and middle-class Atlantans. Doubtless the conflict-free record of the printers reinforced Atlantans' most conservative notions about the proper role of workers' organizations.

## 4. Shoe and clothing manufacturing

Characteristics of shoe and clothing manufacturing in postbellum Atlanta set these enterprises apart from other business concerns examined so far. Writing of shoe manufacturing in the Northeastern states, particularly Massachusetts, from the 1830s into the Civil War, historians have described an industry which expanded dramatically with the coalescence of mechanization and reorganization of work to meet the requirements of mass production. While generally, through the eighteenth century, shoemakers made footwear to order for their customers, changes in the production process occurring early in the nineteenth century altered that line of work in many locales. In Lynn, Massachusetts, for example, shoe manufacturers engaged a corps of craftworkers and a large contingent of unskilled laborers (typically women) in putting-out networks. The invention of the stripper, sole cutter, and adjustable last undermined artisans by making rationalization and skill reduction more feasible. Then, by the middle of the century, widespread introduction of the labor-displacing pegging machine (1857) and the McKay sole-sewing machine (1862) led entrepreneurs to centralize all steps of shoe manufacture in factories for mass production. As early as the 1850s, many of the production units in Lynn were multi-storied, mechanized factories. The new workplace organization and division of labor dictated a transformation of the spatial arrangement on the shop floor. In this transitional phase, commonly the labor force in each production unit in the Northeast expanded from an

1830-level of 50 to100 employees to 300 to 400 by 1850. Following the Civil War, payrolls in single factories sometimes swelled to more than 1,000, mostly low-skilled men and women.[26]

The world of Atlanta's postbellum shoemakers, however, posed a contrast in scale and technology. In 1871, nineteen boot and shoe-making firms operated in the city; ten years later, the number had increased to fifty-five.[27] Within these shops, moreover, the numbers of employees remained small.[28] Marion Gaines's boot and shoe factory employed four adult males in 1880, while, W. E. Guthright hired six. Atlanta's celebrated Eddleman and Brown Company, with its purported state-of-the-art "appliances," had a competitive edge among local shoe producers, with a projected daily output in 1875 of 500 pairs. Yet what was a large operation in Atlanta remained small by comparison to contemporary Northeastern plants.[29]

Shoe manufacturing in Atlanta exhibited a different ownership profile from that of local enterprises already examined. Of the nineteen boot and shoe factories in the city during 1871, blacks owned four, or approximately twenty percent. Black ownership had increased to thirty-three of fifty-five enterprises, or sixty percent, one decade later. Shoemaking workshops doing custom work also doubled, from thirty-nine in 1870 to seventy-eight in 1880. Blacks owned many of these establishments.[30] Evidence by omission supports the likelihood that the employees in these two kinds of businesses were racially segregated and that whites did not work under black employers. Deviations in this pattern certainly would have attracted press attention. Conversely, white employers conceivably hired at least some black workers.

Although wage earners in this line were dispersed across the city and apparently were segregated along racial lines, journeymen in several of the factories successfully carried out a strike action in 1870 which brought them pay increases. Having coalesced specifically "to procure an advance in their wages" without consolidating a broader base, however, their one-time victory proved a limited one. In coverage of the strike, newspaper editors perceived no threat that prompted them to warn the public about the deleterious influences of the union of journeymen shoemakers.[31]

Turning next to Atlanta's needle trades workers, their situation approximately reflects changes in the clothing manufacturing industry nationwide from the 1850s on. Writing about Southern black women's work, historian Jacqueline Jones stresses the extent to which sewing became a vital means for mothers to earn supplemental wages, if they were not single-handedly supporting families. Facing relentless poverty, a large number of Atlanta's black females during parts of their lives conformed to the regional pattern of subcontracting "outside work."[32] Scattered around the city, sewing on a piece-rate basis, these seamstresses merged work with family and neighborhood life. Such social relations of production, of course, differed from those typifying factory situations in the same city. There, even as they labored together in formal work groups, employees remained under the watchful eyes of the factory managers.

Most needle trades workers in Atlanta's garment factories as, indeed, throughout the nation, were women and girls, although men held the key positions. In 1880, for example, the labor force at the Jonas L. Cohen and Emil Selig men's clothing factory, one of the larger clothing factories in the city, comprised some forty workers, of whom thirty-six were women. Jerry Lynch, a men's tailor, regularly employed forty adult workers, of whom thirty were women. At the King hosiery mills, twelve women operated the knitting machines during 1881. Widespread use of the industrial sewing machine, in conjunction with the growing market for ready-made clothing after the Civil War, increasingly opened the labor market to men. Nationally, male participation in the ready-made garment industry actually expanded between 1865 and 1880, while that of females shrank proportionately.[33] Yet, demands of their trade placed a premium on the workers' youth. Manual dexterity and keen eyesight were essential in this line of work. Predictably this group of workers lacked long-term stability. The convergence of reproductive functions, social roles, and economic necessity in the face of recurrent depression-level unemployment resulted in constant labor-force turnover.

The employers' ability to maintain low wages in the industry simultaneously capitalized on and reinforced the high rate of instability. Of enterprises for which data are available, the King hosiery mill mentioned above and the M. Rich and Brothers dry goods store (forerunner of the present Rich's department store chain), which, in 1881, employed forty-five women dressmakers, paid the lowest wages. Women at the King hosiery mill in 1881 received only $2.80 weekly, while those at the Rich company earned from $2 to $7. Unskilled and semiskilled employees of the Georgia Suit and the Cohen and Selig companies, commanded slightly higher daily wages, ranging from 75 to 80 cents; while skilled workers received up to $2. Generalizing from national trends, men holding jobs comparable, or identical, to women's would have received twice the wages paid to female workers.[34] Subsistence-level wages, coupled with management indifference to the monotony and dead-end character of the work, generated little incentive for workers to remain on the job. Such a policy induced women, in particular, to move out of the trade as opportunity arose.

Following the Civil War, the availability and consumption of ready-made clothing increased nationwide. By 1870, most men's clothing fit this category, supplanting the market for custom-made items. A corresponding change in the marketing of women's clothing did not materialize until the 1880s. Mass marketing of ready-made clothing was both the motivation for and the product of the invention of tools for cutting multiple layers of fabric in one operation. This technological innovation prompted the establishment of centralized cutting shops operated by skilled men. Once the material had been cut, middlemen transported it to individual homes or to small workshops, where tailors and their families sewed the pieces together. The evolution of foot-powered sewing machines rapidly led to further reorganization of the work process, promoting the proliferation of small workshops where wage earners labored seemingly endless hours with the new machines. As early as 1871, some Atlanta men's clothing stores marketed items sewn in workshops located on the premises. Then, around 1880, introduction across the country of still faster steam-powered sewing machines led to the removal of all sewing machines to larger, more centralized factories with steam plants.[35]

As the locus of work in clothes manufacturing shifted, so the work process in the tailoring, dressmaking, shirtmaking, and undergarment lines changed, especially after the war. Initially, assembling in small workshops scattered around the city, wage earners labored by hand to produce ready-made clothing. At this early stage, as they had before the war, workers mastered all steps of manual garment cutting, seam stitching, buttonhole making, and button sewing, as well as of conducting business. Such specialization as did prevail channeled women into working with lighter fabrics for underclothing, while men concentrated on heavier materials used for outer garments.[36]

With broad utilization of the sewing machine and changes in the cutting technique, workplaces dispersed further. Whether black women working as seamstresses developed relations with their white counterparts, all being similarly dispersed in residences throughout the city, remains a matter of speculation, in the absence of specific evidence. Mechanization of sewing, however, definitely expanded women's roles in the production process, as they commenced working with all weights of fabric.

Such small gains for females in the needle trades were offset by losses on other levels. That male roles changed even more swiftly threatened the women's position in the labor market. Furthermore, as sewing machines increased productivity, consequently creating more competitive markets, employers lowered the piece-rate paid to workers. Profit margins then rose accordingly. When women could not afford to purchase sewing machines, they had few alternatives to renting them from middlemen, often at exorbitant rates. Finally, poor lighting, inadequate ventilation, long hours, and perpetually declining piece rates were common in these workshops. Reorganization of the work process also led to the division of production steps into the most elementary operations. As dispensable and interchangeable parts of a high-yield machine, workers no longer learned all stages of the production process, but specialized in intricate repetitive tasks over which they exercised little control.[37]

When entrepreneurs concluded that centralization of production would cost them less than subcontracting through middlemen controlling mazes of sweatshops, and when steam-power technology necessitated relocating sewing machines in large factories, working conditions deteriorated still further. Under constant managerial oversight, the pace of work quickened. As productivity rose, wages fell. Meanwhile, specialization of tasks reached new heights, causing increasing rigidity in the division of labor.[38] Like their counterparts nationally, Atlanta's needle trades workers, confronting an intensified division of labor, deskilling of the work process, production speed-ups, mechanization, and reduced wages, lacked any tradition of class-conscious interracial solidarity at the workplace, a deficit intensified by the high turnover in the heterogeneous labor force.

## 5. Cotton textile manufacturing

When, in 1875, Jacob Elsas started Atlanta's first cotton-products manufacturing plant, the Southern Bag Factory, he set a pattern in hiring practices that had decisive implications for workers in his enterprise, as well as for those in the other mills that would commence operations subsequently. Within five years, his company had a payroll with 100 to 160 workers. Between one-half and two-thirds of these were women and children. One year later, in 1881, Elsas expanded the work force, hiring 100 more women.[39] Females also predominated among wage earners in Hannibal Ingalls Kimball's Atlanta Cotton Factory. When, in 1879, that company advertised for operatives, 1,000 women responded. Most were turned away, since only 250 to 300 women, men, and children were hired.

But demand quickly boosted the cotton factory's production, and by 1880 the payroll had expanded to 500 workers.

Initially, these factories refused to employ blacks. Across the postbellum South, profits from the labor of white women and children in such textiles mills were high enough that, in most cases, the owners did not attempt to lower wages for whites by threatening or actually introducing blacks at still lower rates. This policy also allowed employers to claim publicly that in their employment practices, they took to heart the interests of Confederate widows and children working at the mills. Only subsequent industrywide shrinkages of profit margins created pressures for changes in local hiring practices by 1881, when sixteen blacks entered this line of work against the wishes of white employees.[40] Shortly after the International Cotton Exposition, held in the city during late 1881, the Exposition Cotton Mill opened on a grander scale. Several hundred workers tended the plant's 20,000 spindles.[41]

Workplace conditions and production processes shaped the perspectives of wage earners and their families. Fragments of information about Elsas and May's Southern Bag Company, in its first location at Pryor and Mitchell streets, show that a minority of white males dominated skilled positions for which, in 1880, they received average daily wages of $2.50. However, the majority of wage earners—women and children—earned approximately $0.60 per ten-hour shift. When Jacob Elsas later built the imposing Fulton Bag and Cotton Mill alongside the Georgia Railroad, he expanded and intensified the same work process.[42] A similar relationship prevailed at Kimball's short-lived Atlanta Cotton Factory, where women generally were assigned to the weaving, carding, and spinning rooms. Spinning room wages averaged one-half to two-thirds those in other departments for the same eleven and one-half-hour day. Men occupied the skilled positions at the plant, reinforcing the patriarchal structure of society at large, and company regulations forbade workplace contact across gender lines. The effect intensified isolation on the job in the name of enlightened management.[43] The trend carried over to the Exposition Cotton Mill, as well, where 20,000 spindles provided employment for a large contingent of workers, mostly women and none black. Employment was geared to exploit the seemingly inexhaustible supply of women and girls who presumably were eager to work in low-wage positions as unskilled machine tenders.[44]

Low wages, structurally induced divisiveness, and poor physical working conditions assured that desperation and alienation hounded cotton mill workers. A reporter for the *Atlanta Constitution* in 1879 attributed

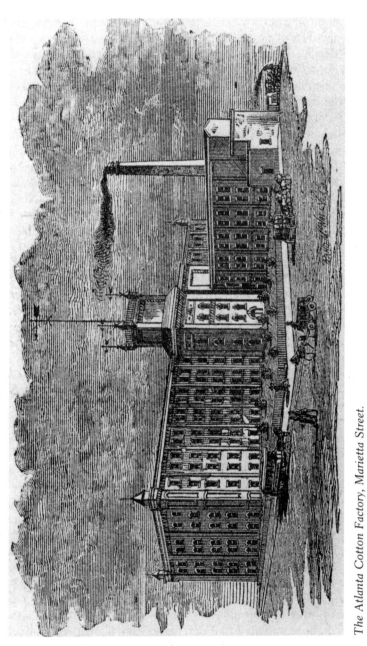

*The Atlanta Cotton Factory, Marietta Street.*
From E.Y. Clarke, *Atlanta Illustrated, Atlanta*

the financial woes of the Atlanta Cotton Factory to the slothfulness and undependability of employees of the establishment, "who come three or four days in the week and stay away the rest of the time." A management representative of the firm carried the analysis further, claiming that "a girl will come to the mill for work. She will work a few days, and then get tired of it." The root cause, according to this analysis, was that " 'they actually seem to have no idea of work—as the women of the north understand it.' " The pandemic despair among workers in cotton manufacturing, however, suggests that systemic rather than pathological factors governed the social relations of production. The outcome typically manifested itself in high turnover and absence of collective identification within the labor force. Thus, the *Constitution* reporter noted that the factory official "had on his books over three times as many operatives as he now has at work, but they have shifted and changed and started and stopped, until scarcely any of the original force is left."[45]

The mill owners' capacity to extract profits from the labor force depended, in part, on their abilities as capitalists to manipulate the labor market, so that employees would never establish the basis for collective action. When workers on the job posed a threat to normal operations, supervisors typically ousted the dissidents, who were replaced by newcomers, all part of a seemingly unending and ever-increasing flow from the fields to the factory.[46]

## 6. Straw goods manufacturing

Straw goods manufacturing, or more precisely, the production of straw sunbonnets, provided a major source of employment for postwar women laborers. Morris Wiseberg's sunbonnet factory, the first such local enterprise, grew out of his wholesale millinery business, established around 1865. By 1880, he employed between 72 and 90 workers, the great majority of them women. The low wages Wiseberg paid his workers (averaging 60 cents for laborers and $1.25 for skilled workers, per ten-hour shift) together with capital investment of $6,000 presumably assured Wiseberg a satisfactory rate of profit.[47] Jonas and Jacob Selig and A. Louis Sondheimer, partners in the Southern Sun Bonnet Factory, also realized substantial profits. The earliest records of this company show that in 1879 some 60 white females operating sewing machines in a large hall assembled straw hats, while still others worked at home on a piece-rate basis. By 1880 the company's labor force numbered 130, of whom all but 5 were women. In 1881, the payroll included 140 women. During these years, the locus of production shifted to private homes and small workshops with sewing machines. Competition intensified in 1881 with the establishment of the Wellhouse and Fleischel sunbonnet factory, which also adopted the putting-out system. Seemingly, then, ignorance of the adverse conditions under which these women worked underlay the blithe observation of an *Atlanta Constitution* reporter that, "the girls [at Seligs and Sondheimer's Southern Sun Bonnet Factory] seemed to be happy and made the sewing machines join in the chorus of their merry songs."[48]

## 7. Paper box manufacturing

Another major source of employment for women was the paper box industry. J. M. Willis and W. S. Bell started the first such factory in conjunction with their planing mill. In 1873, thirty to forty employees, whose gender cannot be ascertained, operated this steam-powered plant. However, an 1876 advertisement for "five girls" to work at the paper box factory on Broad Street suggests that female participation had been a factor from the outset. In 1879, women comprised the largest component in the labor force of the F. G. Hancock Box Company, a later entrant into the industry.[49]

Information on the racial composition of the labor force in paper box production in postbellum Atlanta is not available. By the early twentieth century, though, black women regularly sought employment in those factories because of the comparatively high wages such work afforded them.[50]

# Food Processing

## 1. Bakeries

Throughout the Reconstruction period, food processing with a combined labor force of hundreds of workers figured prominently in Atlanta's industrial economy. Hardly had the war ended when a few companies undertook baking, cracker manufacturing, and candy production. By 1875, over two dozen plants performed these operations.[51] The scale and nature of production in these enterprises varied widely, both with the individual entrepreneur's access to capitalization, and the unevenness in the application of technological and procedural innovations. Thus, within one city, Mrs. N. E. Anderson's small confectionary coexisted with larger

*The Sugar Creek Paper Mills.*
From E.Y. Clarke, *Atlanta Illustrated*, Atlanta

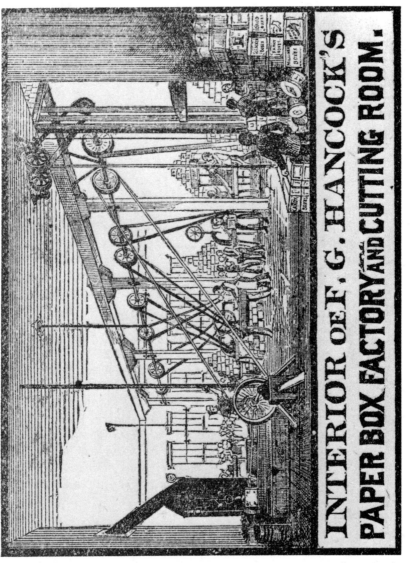

*Interior of F. G. Hancock's Paper Box Factory and Cutting Room.*

From E.Y. Clarke, Atlanta Illustrated, Atlanta

enterprises, including the H. Lewis bakery and cracker factory and F. E. Block's candy factory, which grew steadily until, early in the twentieth century, it ranked as the largest candy producer in the South.[52]

Nationally, the baking industry had been in rapid transformation. The Civil War had stimulated technological innovation and boosted production, increasing the output of crackers. Improved ovens along with mechanical mixers, rollers, and dough cutters became fixtures in cracker factories. Packing, however, remained a manual operation until about 1900.

In Atlanta, the H. Lewis steam bakery was extensively mechanized, but twelve to fifteen women packaged the crackers. Laboring on piece-rate, average daily earnings ranged from 25 cents to $1. During 1881, the G. W. Jack cracker and candy company also hired ten to twenty female cracker packagers, at daily wages of 40 cents to $1.25.[53] The low average of cracker packers' wages suggests that blacks held some of these jobs. While examples are few, in the local baking industry, color did not categorically preclude occupational mobility for blacks, as the case of Aaron Perry exemplifies. Born a slave in Columbus, Georgia, Perry moved to Atlanta in 1876. Taking a job at the Jack and Holland candy and cracker factory, Perry set about learning the baking trade. His expertise eventually led the management to promote him to foreman baker. Perry's advancement into the skilled position of baker was atypical. Yet his career indicates that at least some blacks held jobs in the baking industry.[54]

While cracker manufacturing evolved into a mechanized industry, technological innovation seems scarcely to have affected bread production. Surveying the industry at the turn of the century, William Panschar observed that "seventy-eight percent of the bakeries in the United States in 1899 had four or fewer employees, indicating the continued existence of the small-family handicraft bakeshop. Most of them had only grown from their 1850 level to the extent of hiring an extra hand or two." Seemingly the bakeries in Atlanta producing bread for local consumption did not deviate from this pattern.[55]

## 2. Candy production

Generally, candy production paralleled cracker manufacturing in employment practices and labor-force dynamics. Nationally during Reconstruction, among women employed in food preparation, candy makers numbered second only to cannery workers. In Atlanta, between one-sixth and one-third of the workforce was women. At Block's candy factory in 1881, for example, women filled ten to twenty of sixty-five regular positions. During peak periods, white children supplemented the full-timers. Citywide, in 1880, approximately one dozen blacks held jobs in these companies, but no information is extant on the relations of blacks and whites in the industry.[56]

From the end of the Civil War into the early twentieth century, candy manufacturing ranked at the low end of the wage spectrum for factory jobs held by white women. Average daily wages for such employment in 1880 hovered around 75 cents for a nine- to ten-hour day. Skilled workers fared better on average daily wages, which ranged from $2 to $3. Yet, the irregularity and seasonal character of this work eroded the economic security of even the highest paid candy factory employees. While some of the smaller factories merely varied their hours slightly during the year, other worked more seasonally. The Block candy factory operated at half of capacity during six slack months of the year. Subject to persistent unemployment and tightly circumscribed occupational avenues, the poorest paid workers had fewest options. Thus, for the duration of the century, white women would continue to enter Atlanta's candy factories in substantial numbers.[57] Under these circumstances, factors imposed by management and continually reinforced in the routine of daily life—especially the transitory nature of the sharply divided labor force—weighed heavily against any presumed potential for collective action.

## 3. Meat processing

City government records for 1870 reported twenty-eight licensed butchers, while the 1881 city directory listed forty-five butcher firms.[58] Data are inconclusive as to which enterprises actually slaughtered and packed the animals (converting livestock into fresh meat cuts), and which merely prepared already dressed meat for retail sales. Some firms certainly handled animals on the hoof in their company pens.[59] But there are no indicators to facilitate a breakdown of information about the butcher workers. Whether in those local shops, skilled butchers slaughtered and dressed meat with the assistance of low-skilled laborers (as was the case in Chicago), or performed their tasks in teams comprised exclusively of skilled butcher workers, is not clear.[60] That the several local butcher firms differed widely in the number of employees points to the variety in their operations. The Sparks, Tye and Company, formed in 1874, employed twenty-four workers to maintain animals in pens on the premises, slaughter livestock, and prepare the products as fresh cuts.[61] Jacob Preis started his company in 1880 with only two paid employees. J. N. Hall's slaughterhouse and meatpacking plant, by contrast, operated in 1880 with twenty employees.[62] Among local butchers, in 1870, at least one was a black man. Ten years later, fourteen blacks identified themselves on the census as butchers.[63] Whether they ran shops that served black customers exclusively, or worked with whites in the larger packinghouses remains unclear. Yet it seems likely that skilled butchers worked in close contact with unskilled employees. Because the census generally used only the designation "laborer" to identify such workers, information is not forthcoming about the racial composition of the lower-rank workers in the industry, obscuring details about social relations at the workplace. Yet, the case of thirteen-year old Chester Pace, a black male who the census enumerator uncharacteristically noted "works at meat market," indicates the high probability for contact across skill lines among meat-processing workers.[64]

Given the range in the operational scale of these plants, not surprisingly the working conditions varied widely. At the Preis meatpacking company, the two male employees regularly worked sixteen-hour shifts. Wage rates were low, a skilled worker averaging $1 per day, and a laborer only 50 cents. Workers at the Hall packing house fared somewhat better. For ten-hour stints laborers earned 85 cents, and skilled workers $2 per day. Employment at the Hall plant, however, lasted only four months a year.[65]

From the 1870s onward, the work process in Atlanta's larger packing houses apparently changed gradually. Increasing division of labor and specialization followed the precedent established in Cincinnati's pre-Civil War plants. In fact, the more modern, profit-oriented Atlanta companies may have aggressively pursued policies of task specialization and division of labor, though the extent of change could not have been so drastic as in Chicago, during the closing decades of the nineteenth century, as analyzed by David Brody:

> Now it was carried forward to the most minute degree. The packers ... surveyed and laid off the animal like a map, apportioning to each workman a tiny part of the total operation. There were, for example, 78 different occupations in the beef-killing gang of 157 men at one Chicago plant.

In Atlanta during the 1870s, the less extensive division of labor and the smaller scale of production insured that skilled butchers and subordinate workers (both blacks and whites) developed more personalized, though hierarchical, working relationships. On occasion, this rapport may even have transcended the formal confines of the primary work-group relationship, particularly among workers of the same race. In the less highly capitalized and industrialized Atlanta packinghouses, too, workers certainly could not have been so tyrannized by technology, skill dilution, and assembly-line techniques as were their counterparts in Chicago.[66] Accordingly, Atlanta's skilled meatpackers, who controlled the pace of production, interacted more extensively with other wage earners in the industry than was possible in the highly mechanized Chicago packinghouses.

## Construction

Several thousand construction workers rebuilt Atlanta after the Civil War and facilitated the city's expansion through the 1880s and beyond. Within the broad occupational category "building trades workers" fit a variety of skilled craftworkers: carpenters; plasterers; cabinetmakers; slaters; stone cutters; and brick, stone, and rock masons.[67] The semiskilled included painters, brickmolders, mortarmakers, and terra-cotta workers. Helpers and craftworkers' apprentices also counted as semiskilled. Hod carriers were among the most numerous of the unskilled workers. Characteristic of the construction industry, shifting demand for large crews of day laborers caused sharp fluctuations in the numbers of the unskilled workers so engaged.

Predictably, blacks had a high profile as building trades workers at all skill levels. Of these, laborers were most numerous. Skilled black construction workers, numbered 313 and 447 in the 1870 and 1880 censuses, respectively. Over 200 were carpenters. Brickmakers numbered around 50, and several dozen more worked as plasterers and painters. Because the prospects for a continued boom in construction work in Atlanta were so favorable, black building trades workers benefited from greater security than freedpeople in other sectors of the labor force.[68]

Construction projects around the city varied in type, each having particular specifications and circumstances. Thus, building trades workers engaged on large projects in the public and private sectors sometimes joined crews numbering in the hundreds to erect troop barracks, build roads, construct public facilities, and put up hotels. At other times, they freelanced on small-scale, short-term jobs for individuals. James Brown, a black carpenter, for example, worked alone for three to four weeks in 1873 building shelves and ladders for Samuel P. Richards, a local stationer.[69] Certainly lesser-skilled workers looked for jobs on a pickup basis. It is not clear, however, whether most higher-skilled workers found jobs in that same fashion, by virtue of personal connections with other workers, and through advertisements, or whether they had comparatively steady employment by their attachment to the city's several contracting companies.[70]

In any case, wages remained relatively constant throughout the period. Unskilled streetworkers on the city's 1865 payroll earned a flat $1 per day. Unskilled laborers hired to assist in construction of an American Missionary Association school in Atlanta during 1869 were budgeted for 75 cents per day. Semiskilled workers were scheduled to received $1 to $1.75 daily. Carpenters and masons commanded daily wages of $2 from the association. By this scale, Thomas Goosby's daily earnings of $1.50, as a black carpenter employed during 1866 on several of the city's larger construction projects, were standard. Collin Brown, another black carpenter working on the Atlanta Freedmen's Bureau hospital during 1867, also fared well. At the close of the decade, laborers earned 50 to 80 cents daily, with 75 cents as an average. Skilled building-trades workers even realized a slight increase in average earnings, their daily pay ranging from $1.50 to the $3 offered by the Lynch and Lea company.[71] Once again, these sharp gradations in pay according to skill levels reinforced structural hierarchy in the work process.

Yet, unemployment constantly threatened building trades workers, undermining security even for skilled workers and worsening the lot of the low-paid wage earners, whose numbers expanded with the continual rural-to-urban population movement. By nature, construction work was more or less seasonal. Although some contracting firms in the city operated full-time year around, others, such as the Longley and Robinson firm, with a labor force of 125 men, functioned on ten-month cycles. Laborers employed by this company for 75 cents daily could ill afford long layovers between jobs. Diminished work opportunities resulting from economic slumps, such as characterized Atlanta immediately after the war and during the depressed 1870s, struck all the laborers, and even the craftworkers, hard. For blacks, the situation proved particularly acute because they had fewer employment options than whites. Lamenting circumstances during 1867, Reverend Frederick Ayer of the American Missionary Association wrote:

> Quite a number [of white property holders] have suspended building
> and are deferring executing plans of improvement in the city. Therefore
> their [sic] is far less demand for labor than before, and many cannot pro-
> cure employment. . . . In connexion [sic] with this there is a great scarcity
> of money and again owing to an unusual amount of rainy and cold
> weather—but little outdoor work has been done for a week or two and pro-
> visions are scarce and high. . . . Landlords are pressing the poor at the same
> time to pay their rents—and the poor people are at their wits end to find
> out how to meet their pressing necessities.[72]

Such insecurities added tension to social relations at the workplace.
Individual wage earners were forced into competition with one another,
each seeking to insure employment by outperforming all co-workers. On
sites where 75, 150, or 500 men worked together, a complex division of
labor molded the diverse wage earners into an interdependent unit.
Customarily, the supervisor exercised general oversight, while the foreman regulated how subordinates carried out work assignments and controlled pacing, at the same time that he participated as a member of the
work crew. Consequently, the relationship of the foreman to the craftworkers, apprentices, and helpers assumed a particularly personal character. Because construction tasks were organized along trade lines,
workers in one trade generally viewed other crafts as equal to their own,
and every component job as necessary to the project. Within each trade,
however, hierarchy dictated the pecking order of job assignments. By
virtue of their owning the tools of their crafts, journeymen maintained
considerable autonomy. Confident and proud of their skills, they functioned with only loose employer supervision, the former usually viewing
the latter with respect rather than with deference. Once hired by the con-
tractor, apprentices, helpers, and laborers, working in teams, came under
the supervision of the journeymen as they performed heavy labor.

In this relation, however, an inherent conflict of interest between the
journeymen and their helpers and apprentices ebbed and flowed, depending on circumstances. The persistent problem of skill dilution, which
threatened to lower wages in unorganized communities like Atlanta,
would only be resolved for the craftworkers with formation of building
trades unions powerful enough to enforce union or closed shops,
enabling members to dictate work rules favorable to their own interests.
At the same time, with the high population turnover in Atlanta, at least
some of these hired on any particular project likely envisioned their stay
in the city as temporary and their interactions with other workers as tran-

sitory. These factors, combined with the short duration of most construction jobs, caused instability in the social relations of these workers. Such stresses notwithstanding, however, the organization of the work process around crews performing interdependent tasks promoted a counter tendency of workers cooperating.[73]

Approximately 200 to 250 blacks worked as journeymen carpenters in Atlanta during Reconstruction. Some were employed on construction projects involving dozens, or even hundreds, of workers. Among these were Collin Brown and Thomas Goosby, referred to above. Other skilled black construction workers, including slaters, cabinetmakers, plasterers, and stonecutters, as well as rock, brick, and stone masons, worked on large and small jobs. Determining how these black journeymen functioned with white construction workers, however, remains problematic. Contemporary newspapers indicate that whites and blacks worked on common construction sites, though specifics as to the racial composition of work gangs are lacking.[74]

Thus, it remains unclear whether black journeymen were segregated in all-black work crews or participated in racially mixed units. Given the setting, it seems probable that the latter situation prevailed, since, if black craftworkers had exerted control over whites working under them, protest would have been widespread. There is no record of such protests. Certainly the obverse, that of blacks, even as craftworkers, laboring under whites, frequently occurred, as in the case of Cicero Finch, who labored in Atlanta on shovel and wheel-barrow gangs. Later he assisted in installing a water pump in the Kimball House hotel, probably under white supervisors. Subsequently, Finch set out to master the skills of plastering.[75] Equally enigmatic is the information about social relations among laborers and helpers. Once again, the situation suggests that social interaction between blacks and whites on the building site would have been confined to specific task-related exchanges. Certainly, however, within their own racial groupings, black and white construction workers respectively formed bonds on the job, which in some circumstances carried over outside of the job, perhaps into a distinctly race-conscious variety of working-class cultural experience.

Laborers were most vulnerable to the effects of fragmentary social relations in construction work. Lacking skills with which to bargain in labor-management relations left them in a weak position in this craft-dominated industry. Moreover, polarization among black and white laborers compounded the effects of division along skill lines. Thus, in

April 1871, when the city council rebuffed Atlanta streetworkers who re-
quested a wage increase, the committee of petitioners dissolved for want
of a basis for sustained unity.[76]

Even the early efforts at unionization of the higher-rank building
trades workers met with only fleeting success. The fact that merchants
and residents hastened to rebuild the city initially created a favorable job
market after the war, at least for the skilled workers. Taking advantage
of the favorable opportunity, skilled workers made efforts to organize.
Only fragmentary information survives on the Carpenters and Joiners'
Association, one of the first such bodies. In 1869 and 1870, advertisements and notes in local newspapers encouraged "mechanics," to attend
meetings of that association. The designation of W. H. Frizzell and N.
A. Boutell, both master carpenters, as presidents during 1869 and 1870
indicates the working-class composition of the group. Seemingly, this
short-lived organization served its membership principally as a mutual-
aid/benevolent society, without securing any control over wages and
working conditions.[77] Nevertheless, those who joined organized along
craft lines. The absence of any race-baiting editorials in the local
Democratic press makes clear that blacks did not join.

Once in motion, the dynamics of racial exclusion limited the options
of all Atlanta's construction workers, as two incidents in the midst of the
depression of the 1870s illustrate. Threatened with a fifteen-percent wage
cut, black and white building trades workers erecting a U.S. Customs
House walked off their jobs together in August 1875. In response, the
superintendent hired strikebreakers, some if not all of whom were black,
and attempted to resume the project. Initially, black strikers appealed to
racial pride in trying to convince the black strikebreakers to honor the
job action. When at least two scabs refused to honor these entreaties, a
fight ensued. Atlanta police reacted swiftly. Intervening not merely to restore order, but to reassert the employer's prerogatives over the labor
force, the police apprehended the striking black workers. This state
action fatally weakened the strike.[78] Some white strikers may long have
remembered the interracial solidarity their fellow black strikers exhibited
in 1875. The other image of blacks as strikebreakers, however, probably
had a more lasting impact on white workers because it reaffirmed their
deeply rooted racial antagonisms.

Scarcely a year later, in June 1876, hod carriers and their assistants—
all probably black—struck their employer while building the cotton factory. This job action, the *Atlanta Constitution* smugly informed readers,

"lasted about ten minutes." The employer immediately hired replacements who were more compliant with management aims. In this situation, however, more than the employer's will to defeat the strikers was at issue. Though the work of hod carriers was critical to the construction project, its unskilled character assured that the wage earners were readily replaceable. Only with the support of skilled workers could the lesser-skilled hod carriers have achieved their goals in striking. Yet, as the account made clear, the craftworkers continued their labor, despite the presence of strikebreakers.[79] In this context, then, the principle of solidarity remained narrowly circumscribed in the building trades workers' consciousness.

That such organizations as the Carpenters and Joiners' Association perpetuated craft divisions had telling effect. Stratified at the workplace by race and skill levels, employees faced major obstacles in mounting effective job actions in a hostile setting, especially when they could not count on the cooperation of strategically situated fellow workers. Then, when they did attempt to strike, the narrow vision of collective unity to which they adhered left them vulnerable to management manipulation. Even when, in the late 1880s, building trades workers formed more powerful craft locals and joined national trade unions, their internal divisions, particularly on the matter of organizing blacks in separate locals, rendered them susceptible to management counteroffensives.[80]

The divisiveness of lesser-skilled building trades workers, as well as that of craftworkers, weighed against the interests of all wage earners in the industry. While occupational safety, regularity of employment, and job-related disabilities, as well as wages, remained central concerns of construction workers in the period, organization, whether along industrial or craft lines, languished in part because of the divisive impact of race.

## Service Industries

A significant portion of Atlanta's wage earners engaged in service trades as hotel, restaurant, and laundry workers, sales clerks, and domestic servants. While the circumstances of their lives seldom attracted the attention of contemporaries, a schematic overview casts light on the work processes and social relations in this sphere of the local economy.

## 1. Hotel and food service workers

As a semblance of routine life returned to Atlanta after the war, four to five modest hostelries served the city. Then, in 1866, the National Hotel opened, featuring a billiard hall, bar, and restaurant, as well as sleeping quarters. Four years later, the luxurious 300-room Kimball House opened, followed by the Markham House in 1881.[81] Meanwhile, in 1870, Atlantans patronized several restaurants and some fifty saloons. By 1881, there were twenty-one restaurants, seven of which catered to a black clientele principally, and sixty-six saloons, several of which were centers of black social life.[82]

These establishments provided jobs for hundreds of Atlantans. Across the city, a majority of blacks so employed worked as cooks. Dozens more were waiters and barroom workers, and live-in "servants." Blacks, however, did not monopolize hotel food-service jobs, as operations of the Kimball House kitchen and dining room during 1880 showed. The hotel's head chef, baker, and several female pantry helpers were white. Many of the kitchen helpers were black, including one who had advanced to assistant baker. On the job, kitchen workers had to interact closely with one another. A crew of twenty black waiters served customers.[83]

Both blacks and whites worked in other service jobs as well at the Kimball House during 1880. White administrators supervised the housekeeping and custodial crew, composed mostly of black women, although Irish-immigrant women may have held some of these jobs. Porters and bellhops, also black, worked under the direction of white clerks at the front desk. A steam laundry formed part of the hotel's plant. Black women apparently predominated among the hotel laundry workers, conventionally one of the lowest-paid urban occupations.[84]

In all these hotel jobs, their work in interdependent crews brought employees into continuous interaction with one another. Furthermore, that the dining room staff at the Kimball House shared a "sleeping room" in their off hours provided circumstances for these workers to develop particularly close social relations. While no comparable descriptions of the city's other hotels survive, newspaper reports reveal that waiters at the Markham House organized social events and their counterparts at the National Hotel demonstrated solidarity in striking for higher wages.[85]

In restaurants not affiliated with hotels, relations among white and black service workers are less clear. While these eateries functioned across the city, even in predominantly black neighborhoods, their small size prompted some observers to label many of them "six by nines."[86] Certainly they operated on a less extensive scale than the hotel dining rooms.

## 2. Domestics, laundry workers, and washerwomen

Of service workers in the city, domestics and washerwomen were among the most amorphous groups, a function of this work that had no educational, training, or apprenticeship requirements and was decentralized in character. From the end of the war through the turn of the century, black women, numbering at least 814 in 1870 and 1,414 in 1880, dominated the domestic service category. At the same time, they accounted for over forty percent of all black service workers in 1870, and just under thirty percent ten years later.[87] In their total numbers and in proportion to the labor force, then, black female domestic laborers comprised a formidable segment of the local workforce. Their varied backgrounds and the range of their experiences on the job, however, insured that black domestics remained a heterogeneous element.

Charges whites often made concerning the proclivity of blacks to laziness and irresponsibility notwithstanding, these women performed strenuous labor. Typical work routines involved hauling water and fuel, food preparation and service, and house cleaning. Domestics also washed and ironed their employers' laundry, often while tending children.[88]

After the Civil War, breaking with their slave past, blacks resisted living with white families. To take living quarters where they worked tended to undermine their autonomy and facilitated a dynamic whereby their work shifts would expand at the employers' whim. Separation of work and residence permitted the women to preserve their own family life in a nurturing atmosphere. Contrary to practices in the North, where servants lived with their employers, "living out" was the norm for Southern black domestic workers. Only about fifteen to twenty percent of such workers lived in the homes of employers.

Still, tension in the relationship between employers and domestic workers abounded. Samuel P. Richards, a stationery store proprietor, complained in his diary, for instance, that he and his wife, Sallie, had hired five people in succession, between January and mid-November 1866, because they "soon spoil[ed]." A June entry revealed that he had just fired another in the series because she was "too ignorant and dirty to suit us."[89] Insulated from the immediate support of fellow workers when they confronted their employers' demands, these domestic working women were obliged to rely on their only bargaining power—leaving their jobs—when conditions warranted extreme recourse.

Between 1870 and 1880, the proportion of black females working as domestics, relative to the overall total of black service workers in Atlanta, diminished approximately ten percent (even as the numerical total increased). During the same period, the city's black population as a portion of the whole dropped from forty-six to forty-four percent. Meanwhile, depression drove increasing numbers of black women into the labor force, most of them to work in unskilled and service sector jobs. That same economic crisis, moreover, also affected whites of all classes, forcing many of the moderately affluent among them to reduce household expenditures, which they did by sending laundry to washerwomen as needed, rather than hiring full-time domestic workers. Finally, on the national level, ever wider accessibility of mechanical devices for household tasks reduced the per-household average of domestic workers between 1870 and 1914. The effects altered the lives of Atlanta's middle class beginning in 1870.[90]

Black women comprised the vast majority of laundry workers, as well. In 1870, 842 black women accounted for ninety-eight percent of all such workers. Approximately 13 white women formed the remaining two percent. This ratio continued through 1880 and beyond. The importance of laundries as a source of employment in the black community is further borne out in that washerwomen comprised approximately thirty-nine percent of all black workers in the service sector.[91]

In characterizing the work processes in which these women engaged, distinction must be made between wage earners at commercial laundries and independent washerwomen. Commercial laundries were generally small scale and short-lived. The primitive technology consisted of steam washing machines, manually operated drying racks, heated rollers for pressing, and hand irons heated on hot bricks. Laundry wage earners were low paid and their employment sporadic.[92] Washerwomen, by contrast, operated as independent contractors, working in their own homes. Since these typically were situated in neighborhoods that included others similarly engaged, the washerwomen's experiences assumed a distinctive character. In a day's labor, the worlds of work, family, and community were fluid.

Because, in the past, skilled workers alone had the strategic advantage of indispensability in the work process and experience in organizing, defining grievances, and conducting effective strikes, collective actions these washerwomen undertook, beginning in 1877, stood out as unique. First in May 1877, then in January 1879, and again in July 1880, a small core of washerwomen, who linked their experiences in this work setting and their aspirations, attempted to enforce uniform minimum price standards.[93] These initial efforts, however, met with little success, leaving the women in a competitive situation as they vied for customers accustomed to low rates.

Once again, in the early summer of 1881, the economic squeeze prompted some twenty washerwomen and a few male allies to meet at a church in the predominately black Summerhill neighborhood for the purpose of launching a grassroots union. In this effort, the women may have been inspired by the strength that established unions apparently brought to other workers. Certainly, too, their response bore the mark of African-American culture—manifested in community solidarity and church-centeredness—they and other freedpeople in the city had nurtured since the war.[94]

Organizers immediately appealed to black ministers to support these women's efforts. Through informal networks and the public endorsements of several black churches, the nascent union quickly developed popular support. Within days, 3,000 women joined, raising a strike fund of $300. A strike was called in mid-July 1881. Strikers demanded a uniform rate of one dollar per dozen pounds of wash. Since most women did washing at home among neighbors, while they simultaneously cared for their families, it seems likely that this strike attracted widespread community support among blacks.

White Atlantans, however, were outraged. The very order of their society seemed to be under attack. As white employers refused to grant the higher rate, white landlords threatened to raise rents and to evict the strikers from their houses. The municipal government then intervened by proposing to levy business taxes and licensing fees against washerwomen who continued the work stoppage. Arrests of strikers for disorderly conduct coupled with stiff fines of $5 to $20, or time on the city chain gang, intensified pressures on the strikers. Reportage of the strike in the local press stopped abruptly at this time. Without a clear indication of the strike's resolution, historians have speculated about the probable outcome. Some have suggested the local newspapers likely fell silent on the matter when the washerwomen withstood the attacks of employers and local authorities and won concessions. According to the alternative view, the strike probably failed because of insurmountable opposition.[95] Whichever scenario ended the strike, this action must have raised the prospect that through collective endeavors, workers could improve their lives.

## 3. Retail sales clerks

With diversification of the local economy, during the 1870s, white women began to enter retail sales work. On a small scale, they contributed to the rising trend of female participation in the category of sales clerks. Nationally, between 1870 and 1890, their numbers increased tenfold from 10,000 to 100,000. Contemporaries noted that these women ranged from teenagers to young women, but also included "many middle aged ladies."[96]

Employment situations for Atlanta sales clerks varied widely—small numbers working in each of several dry goods stores, while at Regenstein and Kurtz's yardage store, thirty-five women were employed.[97] Because clerking had higher status as a female occupation than factory labor, even though earnings were about equal, competition for clerking positions was intense. An Atlanta newspaper noted in 1878 that in response to one advertisement announcing openings for six female clerks, over fifty applied. "There are hundreds of girls in Atlanta," the reporter commented, "who would like to get places of this sort at even the lowest average of wages." Atlanta employers boasted of paying the female clerks half of the amount men earned in similar positions.[98]

## The Rise and Decline of the National Labor Union in Atlanta

At the same time that Iron Molders' Union business took William Sylvis to the South in 1869, his concurrent position as president of the National Labor Union (NLU) also gave brief rise to an organizational drive in Atlanta. So it was that in mid-March 1869, Sylvis and his traveling partner, NLU vice-president Richard Trevellick, introduced Atlantans to the cooperativist/socialist goals of the NLU—a vision contrasting sharply with the more familiar tenets of orthodox craft unionism.

Speaking for two hours on "the condition of our country, the wants and rights of labor, and the design and object of the N.L.U.," Trevellick drew a full house at the Atlanta City Hall. One newspaper reporter observed that the audience of men and women received Trevellick warmly. Subsequent events suggest that the organizers had made a favorable initial impression on Atlantans. Several nights later, "quite a number of names were enrolled" in a newly formed "Labor Union" convened in the City Hall.[99] The absence of follow-up stories in the local sources, however, indicates that the career of this NLU-sponsored "Labor Union" was short-lived. That fact is not surprising, in light of the prevailing values in the city.

Historian David Montgomery characterized the NLU, at its inception in 1866 and for its ensuing ten-year existence, as "a series of annual congresses at which each union, trades assembly, national union, eight-hour league, and other association striving for 'amelioration of the condition of those who labor for a living' was entitled to send representatives."[100] As leaders, Sylvis and Trevellick sought to align the NLU with the distinctly radical artisan republican ideological tradition which championed artisans, like self-sufficient yeomen farmers, as the backbones of society. Programmatically, the NLU embraced producer and consumer cooperatives and land reform to be achieved through the collective purchase of parcels under the Homestead Act. In the field of legislative reform, through its political arm, the National Labor Party, the NLU lobbied for the eight-hour day, the end of convict labor, and a ban on exploitation of women in industry. The NLU also broke new ground in promoting the interests of white women workers across the nation by recognizing them as a significant part of the regular labor force worthy of representation, supporting equal pay for equal work, and advocating their admission to the cigar makers and typographical unions.[101]

These proposals in themselves would not necessarily have alienated Atlanta workers from all employment sectors who stood to gain from organization. Rather, it was on the issue of the admission of blacks that controversy over the NLU erupted in Atlanta and throughout the South, as well as in the North. When blacks entered the nation's labor force as wage earners after the Civil War, trade unions had to respond to emancipation. Either unionists would recruit blacks into their ranks, or those blacks would form a vast pool of potential strikebreakers employers could tap to defeat white workers' organizations. Sylvis and a few other Northern labor leaders tried to impress on the NLU constituents the importance of resolving promptly the issue of the proper relationship between organized labor and black workers. In their pragmatic view—leaving aside assumed racial attributes—black and white producers alike shared common concerns which best could be promoted through craft unionism. Accordingly they advocated admitting blacks to NLU-affiliated unions. At the same time, many of the craftworkers who had formed new locals of national trade unions during the war objected to Sylvis's recommendations, favoring instead a practice that left such matters to the discretion of union locals. Conflict over the issue split the NLU membership in three annual conventions, from 1866 through 1868. Then, in 1869, continued internal pressure by Sylvis, as well as external events relating to the founding of the Republican-leaning Colored National Labor Union, produced a momentary consensus in the NLU for recognition of segregated local black unions. This affiliate status conferred on the black locals the right to representation at NLU conventions.[102] Rather than resolving the ongoing conflicts between black and white workers, though, this legitimation of racial segregation actually exacerbated them.

Thus, when the issue of the proper relationship of blacks to the NLU surfaced in Atlanta, the results alienated all parties concerned. Blacks, being wed to the Republican party in 1869, rejected the NLU as a political organization with little apparent clout that threatened to dilute support for the party of Emancipation. Given the stratification of freedpeople in the local labor force, the equivocal racial policies of the NLU offered blacks nothing tangible.[103] For the white workers, as well, with negative sanctions constantly reinforcing pervasive racist ideology, the ideal of biracial unionism in any guise received no support. That the Labor Union appeared stillborn in Atlanta can hardly be surprising.

This outcome also affected the interests of Atlanta's female labor force. If, in the aftermath of the Labor Union's premature failure, local women workers—none of whom, in 1869, were either cigarmakers or typographers—followed the NLU's advocacy on behalf of women wage earners, they would probably have viewed the federation's initiatives as promoting abstract ideals that remained distant from their daily lives.

## NOTES

1. Tenth Census, Special Schedules of Manufactures; *Atlanta Constitution*, 23 February 1867, 5 September 1878, 7 October 1879, 1 April 1880; (Atlanta) *Daily Herald*, 1 November 1872; Frank O. Butler, *The Story of Papermaking: An Account of Paper-Making from Its Earliest Known Record Down to the Present Time* (Chicago: J. W. Butler Paper Company, 1901), p. 131.

2. Tenth Census, Special Schedules of Manufactures; William H. Harris, *The Harder We Run: Black Workers Since the Civil War* (New York: Oxford University Press, 1982), pp. 18–19.

3. Payroll for January [?] 1864, Fulton Paper Mill Company, William McNaught Papers, AHS; Herbert R. Northrup, *The Negro in the Paper Industry* (Philadelphia: Industrial Research Unit, Department of Industry, Wharton School of Finance and Commerce, University of Pennsylvania, 1969), p. 31.

4. Butler, *Story of Papermaking*, pp. 57, 84, and unpaginated photograph plates; Martha

and Murray Zimilies, *Early American Mills*, p. 226; E.Y. Clarke, *Atlanta Illustrated* (Atlanta: James P. Harrison, 1881), p. xxv.

5. Gutman, *Work, Culture and Society*, pp. 220-23, 224-45.

6. Wilson, *Atlanta As It Is*, pp. 17, 113, 125; *Hanleiter's Atlanta City Directory for 1871*, p. 5; *Sholes' Directory of the City of Atlanta for 1881*, pp. 85, 101.

7. *Atlanta Constitution*, 24 December 1871, 22 April 1873, 5 September 1878, 1 April 1880, 22 September 1880; Tenth Census, Special Schedules of Manufactures; Wilson, *Atlanta As It Is*, p. 17; Thornbery, "Development of Black Atlanta," p. 320.

8. *Atlanta Constitution*, 22 April 1873, 22 September 1880; (Atlanta) *Daily Herald*, 18 December 1872; Clyde and Sally Griffen, *Natives and Newcomers*, p. 163; Wilson, *Atlanta As It Is*, pp. 113, 125-26.

9. Tenth Census, Special Schedules of Manufactures.

10. *Atlanta Constitution*, 24 December 1871, 5 September 1878; Wilson, *Atlanta As It Is*, pp. 113-14.

11. *Atlanta Constitution*, 22 September 1880.

12. Montgomery, "Workers' Control of Machine Production," pp. 492-93; Dan Clawson, *Bureaucracy and the Labor Process: The Transformation of U.S. Industry, 1860-1920* (New York and London: Monthly Review Press, 1980), pp. 71-125.

13. Wilson, *Atlanta As It Is*, pp. 57, 61-63, 143; *Sholes' Directory of the City of Atlanta for 1881*, pp. 104, 129.

14. Wilson, *Atlanta As It Is*, pp. 61, 143; Tenth Census, Special Schedules of Manufactures; *Atlanta Constitution*, 17 February 1876.

15. Tenth Census, Special Schedules of Manufactures.

16. Ibid; United States Department of Labor, *Bulletin of the United States Bureau of Labor Statistics*, No. 209: Alice Hamilton and Charles H. Verrill, "Hygiene of the Printing Trades" (Washington, 1917), p. 57; *Atlanta Constitution*, 8 August 1879, 16 June 1881; Mary Van Kleeck, "Changes in Women's Work in Binderies," *Academy of Political Science, Proceedings* 1 (1910): 27-28; Elizabeth Faulkner Baker, *Technology and Women's Work* (New York: Columbia University Press, 1964), pp. 37-48; Mary Van Kleeck, *Women in the Bookbinding Trade* (New York: Survey Associates, 1913), pp. 20-21, 38-39, 48-49, and 31 photograph plates; Joseph W. Rogers, "The Rise of American Edition Binding," in *Bookbinding in America: Three Essays*, ed. Hellmut Lehmann-Haupt (Portland, Maine: Southwork-Anthoensen Press, 1941), pp. 151-58, figures 47-49.

17. Van Kleeck, "Changes in Women's Work," pp. 27-28, 38-39; Ava Baron, "Women and the Making of the American Working Class: A Study of the Proletarianization of Printers," *Review of Radical Political Economics* 14, no. 3 (Fall 1982): 31-33.

18. Bennetts, "Black and White Workers," p. 157.

19. (Atlanta) *Daily Herald*, 21 February 1873.

20. Thornbery, "Development of Black Atlanta," p. 194; *Methodist Advocate*, 17 November 1869.

21. (Atlanta) *Daily New Era*, 24 August 1870; Charles F. Sabel, *Work and Politics: The Division of Labor in Industry* (Cambridge: Cambridge University Press, 1982), pp. 11, 16.

22. Tenth Census, Special Schedules of Manufactures; *Atlanta Constitution*, 16 June 1880.

23. Ibid.

24. (Atlanta) *Daily New Era*, 18 July 1871; Ashworth, *The Helper*, p. 32; Van Kleeck, "Changes in Women's Work," p. 27.

25. *Atlanta Constitution*, 22 February 1873.

26. Dawley, *Class and Community*, pp. 27–29, 76–96; Baker, *Technology and Women's Work*, pp. 29–30.

27. *Hanleiter's Atlanta City Directory for 1871*, p. 17; *Sholes' Directory of the City of Atlanta for 1881*, p. 105.

28. That the statistics on Atlanta's boot and shoe manufacturing in the aggregated manufacturing censuses of 1870 and 1880 differ substantially from the sum of those operations listed individually by name in the city directories during 1871 and 1881 suggests the limitations on the credibility of the census as a definitive source on such matters as overall size of the labor force and its distribution throughout the industry at the local level. To the extent that these census figures provide at least a clue to the nature of the overall labor-force participation in the industry, they remain tools for use circumspectly. It is logical to assume, furthermore, that the census enumerator did not generally ignore large industrial enterprises in accumulating data on the census schedules. Therefore, in using what fragmentary evidence is available from other diverse Atlanta sources in conjunction with the broad outlines suggested by the census, we can study various facets of the shoe manufacturing industry in Atlanta's economy. United States Census Office, Ninth Census, Part III: *Statistics of the Wealth and Industry of the United States* (Washington, 1872), p. 646; Tenth Census, *Report on the Manufactures*, p. 382.

29. *Atlanta Constitution*, 2 March 1875; Laslett, *Labor and the Left*, p. 61.

30. *Hanleiter's Atlanta City Directory for 1871*, p. 17; *Sholes' Directory of the City of Atlanta for 1881*, p. 105; Thornbery, "Development of Black Atlanta," pp. 222, 318.

31. (Atlanta) *Daily New Era*, 20 September 1870.

32. The manuscript schedules of the population censuses for 1870 and 1880 show only that individual women identified themselves as "seamstresses." Such a job description is ambiguous, as it does not distinguish between traditional tailors, factory workers, those doing mending in their houses, and women performing repetitive specialized tasks in the preparation of ready-made clothes under the putting-out system. Nor are the city directories more precise, with their interchanging of the designation "tailor" and "seamstress." Moreover, particularly in an "outwork" kind of labor, the risk of omissions rises significantly. Population Schedules of the Ninth Census, 1870, Roll 151; Population Schedules of the Tenth Census, 1880, Rolls 147–48; Jacqueline Jones, *Labor of Love; Labor of Sorrow: Black Women, Work, and the Family from Slavery to the Present* (New York: Basic Books, 1985), p. 143; Alice Kessler-Harris, *Out to Work: A History of Wage-Earning Women in the United States* ( New York: Oxford University Press, 1982), pp. 77–80; Thornbery, "Development of Black Atlanta," p. 222; *Sholes' Directory of the City of Atlanta for 1881*, pp. 131–131 1/2.

33. Tenth Census, Special Schedule of Manufactures; *Sholes' Directory of the City of Atlanta for 1880* (Atlanta: A. E. Sholes, n.d.), p. 154; *Atlanta Constitution*, 1 April 1880, 16 June 1881; Kessler-Harris, *Out to Work*, p. 78.

34. *Atlanta Constitution*, 16 June 1881; Tenth Census, Special Schedule of Manufactures; Kessler-Harris, *Out to Work*, p. 78.

35. Baker, *Technology and Women's Work*, pp. 25–27; Laslett, *Labor and the Left*, pp. 101–2; Wilson, *Atlanta As It Is*, pp. 92–93.

36. Kessler-Harris, *Out to Work*, p. 78.

37. Ibid.; Laslett, *Labor and the Left*, pp. 101–2; Barbara Meyer Wertheimer, *We Were There: The Story of Working Women in America* (New York: Pantheon, 1977), p. 155; Baker, *Technology and Women's Work*, pp. 25–26; Thornbery, "Development of Black Atlanta," pp. 29–44.

38. Kessler-Harris, *Out to Work*, p. 78; Baker, *Technology and Women's Work*, pp. 26–27.
39. *Beasley's Atlanta Directory for 1875* (Atlanta: James W. Beasley, n.d.), p. 82; *Atlanta Constitution*, 1 April 1880, 16 June 1881; Tenth Census, Special Schedules of Manufactures.
40. Russell, "Atlanta, Gate City," pp. 158–61; Garrett, *Atlanta and Environs*, 1:909; *Atlanta Constitution*, 19 September 1879, 3 October 1879, 7 October 1879, 20 November 1879; Thornbery, "Development of Black Atlanta," pp. 194, 320; Sir George Campbell, *White and Black*, p. 369; Jaynes, *Branches Without Roots*, pp. 273–75.
41. *New York Times*, 21 July 1881, 3 November 1881, 6 November 1881.
42. *Atlanta Constitution*, 1 April 1880, 16 June 1881; Tenth Census, Special Schedules of Manufactures; Garrett, *Atlanta and Environs*, 1:809.
43. *Atlanta Constitution*, 20 November 1879, 16 June 1881.
44. *New York Times*, 3 November 1881.
45. *Atlanta Constitution*, 20 November 1879.
46. Janiewski, "From Field to Factory," p. 141; Kessler-Harris, *Out to Work*, p. 122.
47. Hertzberg, *Strangers Within the Gate City*, p. 40; Tenth Census, Special Schedules of the Manufactures; *Atlanta Constitution*, 1 April 1880.
48. *Atlanta Constitution*, 11 March 1879, 16 June 1881; Tenth Census, Special Schedules of Manufactures.
49. *Atlanta Constitution*, 20 April 1873, 18 November 1876, 16 June 1881; (Atlanta) *Methodist Advocate*, 6 August 1879; Tenth Census, Special Schedules of Manufactures.
50. United States Department of Labor, Women's Bureau, *Bulletin* No. 22: "Women in Georgia Industries: A Study of Hours, Wages, and Working Conditions" (Washington, 1922), p. 9.
51. *Barnwell's Atlanta City Directory and Stranger's Guide*, pp. 114, 116, 118; *Hanleiter's Atlanta City Directory for 1870*, pp. 4, 5; *Beasley's Atlanta Directory for 1875*, pp. 250, 258, 259, 265; *Sholes' Directory for the City of Atlanta for 1881*, pp. 102, 107, 111.
52. *Beasley's Atlanta Directory for 1875*, p. 259; (Atlanta) *Daily New Era*, 10 October 1871; *Atlanta Constitution*, 20 April 1873; Tenth Census, Special Schedules of Manufactures; Harvey K. Newman, "The Frank Block Case and the Exercise of Presbyterian Church Discipline," *Georgia Historical Quarterly* 68, no. 4 (Winter 1983): 503n.
53. William G. Panschar, *Baking in America: Economic Development* (Evanston: Northwestern University Press, 1956), p. 67; (Atlanta) *Daily New Era*, 10 October 1871; *Atlanta Constitution*, 16 June 1881; Wilson, *Atlanta As It Is*, p. 129.
54. Carter, *The Black Side*, pp. 201–3; Thornbery, "Development of Black Atlanta," p. 319; Hopkins, "Patterns of Persistance" pp. 106, 113.
55. Panschar, *Baking in America*, p. 68; Wilson, *Atlanta As It Is*, p. 129.
56. Baker, *Technology and Women's Work*, p. 49; Tenth Census, Special Schedules of Manufactures; *Atlanta Constitution*, 24 January 1871, 16 June 1881; Thornbery, "Development of Black Atlanta," p. 320.
57. United States Department of Labor, Women's Bureau, *Bulletin*, no. 22, p. 9; Tenth Census, Special Schedules of Manufactures; Baker, *Technology and Women's Work*, p. 49.
58. Wilson, *Atlanta As It Is*, p. 17; *Sholes' Directory for the City of Atlanta for 1881*, p. 106.
59. David Brody, *The Butcher Workmen: A Study of Unionization* (Cambridge: Harvard University Press, 1964), pp. 3–4, 8–9; *Atlanta Constitution*, 26 November 1874.
60. Brody, *Butcher Workmen*, p. 4.
61. *Atlanta Constitution*, 26 November 1874.
62. Tenth Census, Special Schedules of Manufactures.
63. Thornbery, "Development of Black Atlanta," p. 319.

64. Walter Fogel only notes in passing that the meatpacking industry in the South during the nineteenth century remained negligible, and that few blacks were employed therein. Walter A. Fogel, *The Negro in the Meat Industry* (Philadelphia: Industrial Research Unit, Department of Industry, Wharton School of Finance and Commerce, University of Pennsylvania, 1970), pp. 18–19; Population Schedules of the Tenth Census, 1880, Roll 148, p. 193.

65. Tenth Census, Special Schedules of Manufactures.

66. Brody, *Butcher Workmen*, pp. 4–5.

67. During the period, plumbing was not an established trade, particularly in the South.

68. Northrup, *Organized Labor and the Negro*, pp. 17, 20, 26; Spero and Harris, *Black Worker;* p. 16; Thornbery, "Development of Black Atlanta," pp. 318, 319, 321.

69. (Atlanta) *Daily New Era*, 12 March 1868, 6 June 1870, 28 August 1870, 2 September 1870, 6 September 1870, 18 July 1871; Samuel P. Richards Diary, AHS, 15 January 1873.

70. Wilson, *Atlanta As It Is*, p. 17; *Sholes' Directory for the City of Atlanta for 1880*, pp. 415, 417.

71. Minutes of the City Council of Atlanta, Report to the City Council, 7 July 1865, AHS; American Missionary Association, Archives, Georgia Manuscripts, Microfilm Publication, Roll 3, letter 20796 to Rev. E. P. Smith, 22 July 1867; Carter, *The Black Side*, pp. 166–67; Bureau of Refugees, Freedmen, and Abandoned Lands, Records of the Sub-Assistant Commissioner, RG 105, Journal of Orders and Complaints, 15 June 1867, NARA; Tenth Census, Special Schedules of Manufactures.

72. Tenth Census, Special Schedules of Manufactures; Blassingame, *Black New Orleans*, pp. 63–64; American Missionary Association, Archives, Georgia Manuscripts, Microfilm publication, Roll 3, Letter 20617 to Rev. E. P. Smith, 30 March 1867.

73. Herbert A. Applebaum, *Royal Blue: The Culture of Construction Workers* (New York: Holt, Rinehart and Winston, 1981), pp. 22, 25, 60–61, 63–64, 93, 96; Ashworth, *The Helper*, pp. 26, 32.

74. (Atlanta) *Daily New Era*, 19 July 1871; *Atlanta Constitution*, 19 November 1880.

75. Rabinowitz, *Race Relations*, p. 67; Willard Neal, "Interview with Cicero Finch," in *Slave Testimony: Two Centuries of Letters, Speeches, Interviews, and Autobiographies*, ed. John W. Blassingame (Baton Rouge: Louisiana State University Press, 1977), p. 584.

76. *Atlanta Constitution*, 8 April 1871; (Atlanta) *Daily New Era*, 8 April 1871.

77. *Atlanta Constitution*, 4 December 1869; 20 March 1870; (Atlanta) *Daily New Era*, 23 July 1870; Evans, "History of Organized Labor," p. 30.

78. Thornbery, "Development of Black Atlanta," p. 220; *Atlanta Constitution*, 28 August 1875; 31 August 1875.

79. *Atlanta Constitution*, 1 June 1876.

80. Evans, "History of Organized Labor," pp. 29–30, 205; Spero and Harris, *Black Worker*, pp. 18–22.

81. Garrett, *Atlanta and Environs*, 1:921–22; Wilson, *Atlanta As It Is*, p. 66; *Sholes' Directory for the City of Atlanta for 1881*, p. 119.

82. Hanleiter, *Hanleiter's Atlanta City Directory for 1880*, p. 14; *Sholes' Directory for the City of Atlanta for 1881*, pp. 129 1/2, 130; Wilson, *Atlanta As It Is*, p. 17; Thornbery, "Development of Black Atlanta," pp. 205–6.

83. Wilson, *Atlanta As It Is*, pp. 66–74; Population Schedules of the Tenth Census, 1880, Roll 148, pp. 508, 509; (Atlanta) *Daily New Era*, 21 October 1870.

84. Thornbery, "Development of Black Atlanta," pp. 321–22; Wilson *Atlanta As It Is*, pp. 67–68, 73; Population Schedules of the Tenth Census, 1880, Roll 148, pp. 508, 509; *Atlanta Constitution*, 3 March 1881.

85. Garrett, *Atlanta and Environs*, 1:716–17, 921; Wilson, *Atlanta As It Is*, pp. 67–68; *Atlanta Constitution*, 22 November 1877, 29 July 1881; Thornbery, "Development of Black Atlanta," pp. 218–19.

86. *Atlanta Constitution*, 26 March 1875, 20 July 1881.

87. Aggregate census statistics about domestic service workers in Atlanta for 1870 are not available. Several other sources, however, permit reconstitution of the statistical characteristics of this occupational group. Grigsby Wotton and Jerry Thornbery independently compiled figures for the number of black female domestics in the city during 1870, as recorded on the manuscript schedules of the population census of that year. Wotton arrived at the figure of 814, while Thornbery uses the number 834. Adding the more conservative, 814, to Wotton's total of 37 white women domestics, yields a total of 851 black and white female domestics. Accordingly, the 814 black female domestics account for 95.7 percent of all the women working in that line during the year. Furthermore, Howard Rabinowitz argues that in the same census year, over 76 percent of all unskilled jobs in the city were held by blacks. Thus, it follows that in 1870, blacks, particularly females, predominated in this job category. Rabinowitz also demonstrates that 92 percent of black women workers in Atlanta during the 1890 census enumeration were domestics, while 96.5 percent of female domestics were black. Therefore, the pattern of black women prevailing as domestic workers is sustained. Wotton, "New City," p. 221; Thornbery, "Development of Black Atlanta," p. 322; Rabinowitz, *Race Relations*, pp. 63, 65, 66.

88. Diary of Samuel P. Richards, 17 June 1866; (Atlanta) *Daily New Era*, 27 February 1868; David M. Katzman, *Seven Days a Week: Women and Domestic Service in Industrializing America* (Urbana: University of Illinois Press, 1978), pp. 184–202.

89. Population Schedules of the Ninth Census, 1870, Roll 151; Population Schedules of the Tenth Census, 1880, Rolls 147–48; Katzman, *Seven Days*, p. 199; Jones, *Labor of Love*, pp. 127–34; Samuel P. Richards Diary, 15 October 1865, 17 June 1866, 24 June 1866, 17 November 1866.

90. Kessler-Harris, *Out to Work*, pp. 111–13.

91. Wotton, "New City," p. 221; Thornbery, "Development of Black Atlanta," pp. 214–15, 322.

92. Information on laundries in Atlanta during the period is sparse, usually confined to passing mention in local interest columns of the daily newspapers and to inconspicuous notices in the city directories. Apparently, with the exception of the laundry at the Kimball House Hotel, such establishments were short-lived, because they could not sustain themselves in the depression-ridden economy. In addition to the Kimball House laundry, four others have been identified: the Atlanta Steam Laundry (1870), the E. L. & L. M. Steam Laundry Company (1871), the Lucas Laundry (1877), and the Atlanta City Laundry, known also as John R. Gregory's Laundry (1878–1879). (Atlanta) *Daily New Era*, 28 May 1870, 10 December 1871; *Atlanta Constitution*, 28 October 1877; *Sholes' Directory of the City of Atlanta for 1878* (n.p.: A. E. Sholes, n.d.), p. 411; *Norton's Directory of the City of Atlanta for 1879* (Atlanta: Charles Norton and Company, 1879), pp. 202, 416; Wilson, *Atlanta As It Is*, p. 68; Kessler-Harris, *Out to Work*, p. 112.

93. *Atlanta Constitution*, 29 May 1877, 9 January 1879; 29 July 1881; Population Schedules of the Ninth Census, 1870, Roll 151; Population Schedules of the Tenth Census, 1880, Rolls 147–48.

94. McLeod, "Black and White Workers," pp. 244–58, 263–66.

95. *Atlanta Constitution*, 20 July 1881, 21 July 1881, 26 July 1881, 29 July 1881, 30 July 1881, 3 August 1881, 16 August 1881; Thornbery, "Development of Black Atlanta," pp.

214-15; Tera W. Hunter, " 'Washing Amazons' on Strike: A Study of Afro-American Female Laundry Workers in Atlanta in 1881," Seventh Berkshire Conference on the History of Women, Wellesley College, Wellesley, Mass., June 1987, pp. 20-21; Rabinowitz, *Race Relations*, p. 74.

96. Wertheimer, *We Were There*, p. 238; *Atlanta Constitution*, 27 March 1878.

97. *Atlanta Constitution*, 1 April 1880, 16 June 1881.

98. Kessler-Harris, *Out to Work*, pp. 135-41; *Atlanta Constitution*, 27 March 1878.

99. Todes, *Sylvis and the National Labor Union*, pp. 103-4; *Atlanta Constitution*, 7 March 1869, 11 March 1869, 12 March 1869.

100. Montgomery, *Beyond Equality*, p. 180.

101. Grossman, *William Sylvis, Pioneer*, pp. 224-25; Montgomery, *Beyond Equality*, pp. 186-96; Eric Foner, *Tom Paine and Revolutionary America* (London: Oxford University Press, 1976); Eric Foner, *Free Soil, Free Labor, Free Men: The Ideology of the Republican Party Before the Civil War* (London: Oxford University Press, 1970); Wertheimer, *We Were There*, pp. 160-63.

102. Sylvis, "Letters from the South," p. 341; W. E. B. DuBois, *Black Reconstruction in America, 1860-1880* (New York: Atheneum, 1971), pp. 354-58; Herman D. Block, "The National Labor Union and Black Workers," *Journal of Ethnic Studies*, no. 1 (Spring 1973), pp. 15-19; Philip S. Foner, *Organized Labor and the Black Worker, 1619-1973* (New York: International Publishers, 1974), pp. 17-26; Saxton, *The Indispensable Enemy*, pp. 40-43.

103. McLeod, "Black and White Workers," pp. 323-25.

CHAPTER IV

# CONCLUSION

The interplay of many factors—the structure of the local economy, work organization and changes in labor processes over time, and the nature of social relations at the point of production—atomized and polarized Atlanta's workers in the postbellum period. Still, as the overview of diverse local enterprises in the transportation, manufacturing, food processing, construction, and service sectors reveals, the impact of these dimensions varied according to the particular circumstances prevailing in each industry, or even within different workplaces in the same occupation. The convergence of these experiences, on the one hand, and the workers' aspirations and perceptions, on the other, molded their courses of action.

Dynamics in the iron manufacturing, railroading, and printing industries, in particular, promoted working-class collective identity. Presumably some of these workers came to identify themselves as wage earners with distinct interests. Overall, their emerging class consciousness stemming from work experiences followed along skill lines, rendering the craftworkers receptive to nascent trade unionism. Encompassing a wide range of contradictions, this craft-based organizational form crystallized when skilled workers united to resist management efforts to deskill production processes and intensify the division of labor. Craft unionism formed the organizational platform from which craftworkers fought to control the production process and to maintain their semi-autonomous primary work groups. Ironically, in legitimating restrictive policies on entry-level positions, so as to make secure the jobs of skilled workers already employed, craft unionism further isolated the majority of production workers who were not skilled.

In the case of low-skill workers, mobilization was most effective with washerwomen and hotel employees who belonged to well-defined occupational groupings. Their bargaining power derived from their capacity to terminate services on which broad sectors of the general public depended.

Accounting for gender-related skill distinctions in occupations, the sexual division of labor lessened the probability of organization that included women and men across skill and occupational lines within Atlanta's several industries. Moreover, outside the workplace, conventional social and psychological bonds linking women first and foremost to their families, rather than to their wage-earner status, minimized general concern about the strategic advantages of organizing women.[1]

Meanwhile, in the postwar economy and beyond, intense competition at the local and regional levels pitted entrepreneurs across the nation against one another in a fierce battle to maintain profit margins. Correspondingly, the conduct of labor-management relations moved for the first time into the forefront of employers' concerns. The attempt to assure themselves of ample cheap and docile wage earners coincided with the employers' determination to intensify the labor process.[2] This drive among small-scale entrepreneurs and large capitalists alike was as much a driving force in Atlanta as elsewhere. For instance, in 1880, the editor of the *Atlanta Constitution* encouraged the management of the troubled cotton mill to erect housing for female operatives, so as to expand the available labor pool. Such facilities, the editor assured the mill owners, would generate additional profit for the management and assure the routine presence of a "steady and reliable" workforce.[3]

Toward their desired end of imposing on Atlanta an economy characterized by plentiful low-wage and deferential workers, Atlanta's employers balanced paternalism and overt coercion. Throughout the period, in both small and larger enterprises, the workers, particularly the skilled, labored in environments where they sustained close personal relationships with their supervisors, if not with company owners. The resulting intimacy, whether spontaneous or induced, decisively affected labor-management relations.

On more than one occasion, for example, the local press paid tribute to A. T. Finney. This celebrated carriage manufacturer attracted public acclaim as much because his own earlier apprenticeship taught him how to build carriages, as because of his success in business. Able to supervise his thirty to forty employees personally, Finney conveyed the impression of having his workers' interests at heart. That personal quality of their relationship garnered Finney a bonus in December 1872, when his employees presented him with a gold-headed cane to commend him "as an employer and citizen." In bestowing the gift, the spokesperson of the group referred to his co-workers as "independent" and "self-reliant" while delivering a sharp attack on those who rejected capitalism. Finney could hardly have disagreed with those sentiments.[4]

Managers of the Phoenix Planing Mill followed another strategy to woo skilled workers into alliance with their employers. In December 1866, Landsberg and Harris invited their employees to a banquet at the Empire Restaurant. The event was "done up in mastodon style. Turkey, oysters, brandies, noggs, champagnes, etc., played a conspicuous and invigorating part." Whatever expense the mill management incurred may quickly have been recovered, for in response, the workers pledged to work hard in the year ahead and to recommend the mill to the public.[5]

Tales of gold-headed canes, gold watches, and elegant chairs bestowed by workers on their employers, as reported in the daily newspaper, are numerous. To the extent that employees felt obliged to flatter their bosses with gifts to receive advancements, or even to retain their positions, such rites became extortionate. Much of the exchange of tributes, particularly by white skilled workers in postbellum Atlanta, however, seemingly reflected their real ambitions and sincerely expressed the deference they felt toward their employers, whom they may even have envisioned as virtuous fellow "producers."[6]

Conflict, however, was never far below the surface. Therefore, when paternalism faltered in creating a compliant work force, employers throughout the city attempted to dominate the work process through coercion. Such was the strategy of the rolling mill management, which sought to realign the power skilled workers exercised over the production process and repeatedly expressed alarm about the employees' resiliency in confronting management on issues of job control. To crush that opposition, as early as 1875 and again in 1881, the rolling mill management endeavored to coerce the workers at the plant to sign iron-clad agreements renouncing union membership as a precondition of employment, acquiescing in a ban on all collective action among employees, and barring subsequent union affiliation while they were employed at the mill.[7]

In the conscious manipulation of race as a device to polarize workers and undermine the potential for biracial working-class unity on the job and in the community, employers scored their most decisive and far-reaching gains. Throughout the local economy, in small-scale business concerns and in larger operations, struggling entrepreneurs and en-

trenched capitalists alike infused racial discrimination into formal policies and informal practices to control the labor force. Racial inequality
thus shaped all aspects of production relations, from hiring preferences
and job assignments to advancement opportunities and wage differentials. The desired effect materialized as black and white workers repeatedly were forced into direct competition on these matters. Tensions were
to reach the exploding point during job actions, such as those initiated
by white rolling mill and black railroad workers, when management used
black and white strikebreakers respectively to break the work stoppages.

Employer policies of this nature had devastating effectiveness. White
workers would champion restrictions on black entry into skilled positions,
if not the total elimination of blacks from workplaces where whites
labored. Freedpeople seemingly threatened the hold whites had on a
range of jobs. Reinforcing their endorsement of racially discriminatory
employment policies by scabbing against black railroad workers who protested the W&A's policies on accident liability, white wage earners raised
tensions to the critical level. Suspicions black workers harbored about
white wage earners must have seemed well-founded. By intensifying racial conflict at the workplace, employers effectively forestalled any potential threat of united working-class opposition. Black and white workers
alike proved vulnerable to management manipulation.

Despite their own impoverishment, which often rivaled that of the
blacks, whites defined themselves as a privileged caste. So long as this
ideology of white racial supremacy prevailed, no concept of working-class
unity could materialize. Without a strong current of working-class unity,
skilled white male workers in some occupations would resort to narrow
craft-based job-conscious unionism. Other workers, facing unrelenting
employer resistance, would fail in this effort. Divided by rigid functional
differentiation and occupational hierarchy, lesser-skilled workers—black
and white, male and female—remained isolated at the workplace.

## NOTES

1. Christine Stansell, *City of Women: Sex and Class in New York, 1789–1860* (New York: Alfred A. Knopf, 1986), p. 128; Jones, *Labor of Love*, pp. 58, 63–64, 74–78, 112–14, 123–28, 200.

2. John Amsden, "Introduction," in Daniel Guerin, *100 Years of Labor in the USA* (London: Ink Links, 1979), pp. 13–14; Licht, "Nineteenth-Century American Railwaymen," pp. 27–28, 33; Lightner, *Labor on the Illinois Central*, pp. 218–19.

3. *Atlanta Constitution*, 2 January 1880.

4. Ibid., 22 April 1873; Wilson, *Atlanta As It Is*, p. 113; (Atlanta) *Daily Herald*, 18 December 1872, 1 January 1873.

5. (Atlanta) *Daily New Era*, 28 December 1866.

6. Licht, "Nineteenth-Century American Railwaymen," pp. 69–70; Gutman, *Work, Culture and Society*, pp. 232–33; Hopkins, "Patterns of Persistence," p. 3.

7. *Atlanta Constitution*, 21 May 1875; *National Labor Tribune*, 24 September 1881.

# Selected Bibliography

## Archival Materials

*Atlanta Historical Society*

Atlanta. City Clerks Office. Register of Merchants, 1868–1870.

Atlanta. Minutes of the City Council, 1848–1886.

William McNaught Papers, Fulton Paper Mill Company, Payroll, January 1864.

*Duke University, The Perkins Library, Manuscripts Division*

John Emory Bryant Papers.

United States. Bureau of the Census. Ninth Census (1870), Schedule of Social Statistics.

United States. Bureau of the Census. Tenth Census (1880), Special Schedule of Manufactures, Fulton County, Georgia.

*Emory University, Robert W. Woodruff Library, Special Collections*

Atlanta and Westpoint Railroad Company, Payroll, Division No.2, October 1865, Georgia Miscellany Collection.

*Georgia Department of Archives and History*

Western and Atlantic Railroad Collection. Atlanta Division Payroll, January–August 1865.

Western and Atlantic Railroad Collection. Master of Transportation, Communications and Letterbook.

Western and Atlantic Railroad Collection. Superintendent's Record, Outgoing Correspondence.

*National Archives*

Record Group 105, Bureau of Refugees, Freedmen and Abandoned Lands. Records of the Assistant Commissioner for the State of Georgia, 1865–1869. Microfilm copy.

Record Group 105, Bureau of Refugees, Freedmen and Abandoned Lands. Records of the Sub-Assistant Commissioner for the State of Georgia, Atlanta District.

Record Group 105, Bureau of Refugees, Freedmen and Abandoned Lands. Registers and Letters Received by the Commissioner. Microfilm copy.

Record Group 105, Bureau of Refugees, Freedmen and Abandoned Lands. Retained Reports of Attendants Employed at the Bureau of Refugees, Freedmen and Abandoned Lands Hospital, Atlanta.

## Newspapers

*American Missionary*

*Atlanta Constitution*

*Daily Herald* (Atlanta)

*Daily Intelligencer* (Atlanta)

*Daily New Era* (Atlanta)

*Daily Sun* (Atlanta)

*Methodist Advocate* (Atlanta)

*National Labor Tribune* (Pittsburgh)

## Published Sources: Articles

Baron, Ava. "Women and the Making of the American Working Class: A Study of the Proletarianization of Printers." *Review of Radical Political Economics* 14 (1982): 23–42.

Bartley, Numan V. "Another New South?" *Georgia Historical Quarterly* 65 (1981): 119–37.

Berlin, Ira and Herbert G. Gutman. "Natives and Immigrants, Free Men and Slaves: Urban Workingmen in the Antebellum American South." *American Historical Review* 88 (1983): 1175–1200.

Blicksilver, Jack. "The International Cotton Exposition of 1881 and Its Impact Upon the Economic Development of Georgia." *Textile History Review* 1 (1960): 175–94.

Bloch, Herman D. "The National Labor Union and Black Workers." *Journal of Ethnic Studies* 1 (1973): 13–21.

Brownell, Blaine A. "The Urban South Comes of Age, 1900–1940." In *The City in Southern History: The Growth of Urban Civilization in the South*, edited by Blaine A. Brownell and David R. Goldfield. New York: Kennikat Press, 1977.

Davies, Margery. "Woman's Place Is at the Typewriter: The Feminization of the Clerical Labor Force." *Radical America* 8 (1974): 1–28.

Davis, Ronald L. F. "Labor Dependency Among Freedmen, 1865–1880." In *From the Old South to the New: Essays on the Transitional South*, edited by Walter J. Fraser, Jr. and Winfred B. Moore. Westport, Conn. and London: Greenwood Press, 1981.

Dew, Charles B. "David Ross and the Oxford Iron Works: A Study of Industrial Slavery in the Early Nineteenth Century South." *William and Mary Quarterly* 31 (1974): 189–224.

_____. "Disciplining Slave Ironworkers in the Antebellum South: Coercion, Conciliation, and Accommodation." *American Historical Review* 79 (1974): 393–418.

Doyle, Don Harrison. "Urbanization and Southern Culture: Economic Elites in Four New South Cities (Atlanta, Nashville, Charleston, Mobile) c.1865–1910." In *Toward a New South? Studies in Post-Civil War Southern Communities*, edited by Orville Vernon Burton and Robert C. McMath, Jr. Westport, Conn: Greenwood Press, 1982.

Fields, Barbara J. "Ideology and Race in American History." In *Region, Race and Reconstruction: Essays in Honor of C. Vann Woodward*, edited by J. Morgan Kousser and James M. McPherson. New York and Oxford: Oxford University Press, 1982.

Goldin, Claudia. "Female Labor Force Participation: The Origin of Black and White Differences, 1870 and 1880." *Journal of Economic History* 37 (1977): 87–108.

Graziosi, Andrea. "Common Laborers, Unskilled Workers: 1880–1915." *Labor History* 22 (1981): 512–44.

Gutman, Herbert G. "The Reality of the Rags-to-Riches 'Myth': The Case of Paterson, New Jersey, Locomotive, Iron, and Machinery Manufacturers, 1830–1880." In *Nineteenth-Century Cities: Essays in the New Urban History*, edited by Stephen Thernstrom and Richard Sennett. New Haven: Yale University Press, 1969.

Harris, William. "Work and the Family in Black Atlanta, 1880." *Journal of Social History* 9 (1976): 319–30.

Hellwig, David J. "Black Attitudes Toward Immigrant Labor in the South, 1865–1910." *Filson Club History Quarterly* 54 (1980): 151–68.

Hertzberg, Steven. "Southern Jews and Their Encounter with Blacks: Atlanta, 1850–1915." *Atlanta Historical Journal* 23 (1979): 7–24.

Hopkins, Richard J. "Status, Mobility, and the Dimensions of Change in a Southern City: Atlanta, 1870–1910." In *Cities in American History*, edited by Kenneth T. Jackson and Stanley K. Schultz. New York: Alfred A. Knopf, 1972.

Horton, George R. and Ellsworth Steele. "The Unity Issue Among Railroad Engineers and Firemen." *Industrial and Labor Relations Review* 10 (1956): 48–69.

Janiewski, Dolores. "Sisters Under Their Skins: Southern Working Women, 1880–1950." In *Sex, Race, and the Role of Women in the South*, edited by Joanne V. Hawks and Sheila L. Skemp. Jackson: University of Mississippi Press, 1983.

Marks, Carole. "Split Labor Markets and Black-White Relations, 1865–1920." *Phylon* 42 (1981): 293–308.

"The Mill That Began As a World's Fair." *Ties* (1962).

Miller, Randall M. "The Enemy Within: Some Effects of Foreign Immigrants on Antebellum Southern Cities." *Southern Studies: An Interdisciplinary Journal of the South* 24 (1985): 30–53.

Montgomery, David. "Labor and the Republic in Industrial America: 1860–1920." *Mouvement Social*, no. 111 (1980), pp. 201–15.

_____. "Strikes in Nineteenth-Century America." *Social Science History* 4 (1980): 81–104.

_____. "Workers' Control of Machine Production in the Nineteenth Century." *Labor History* 17 (1976): 485–509.

Newman, Harvey K. "The Frank Block Case and the Exercise of Presbyterian Church Discipline." *Georgia Historical Quarterly* 68 (1983): 503–11.

Rabinowitz, Howard N. "Continuity and Change: Southern Urban Development, 1860–1900." In *The City in Southern History: The Growth of Urban Civilization in the South*, edited by Blaine A. Brownell and David R. Goldfield. Port Washington, N.Y.: Kennikat Press, 1977.

Rogers, Joseph W. "The Rise of American Edition Binding." In *Bookbinding in America: Three Essays*, edited by Hellmut Lehmann-Haupt. Portland, Maine: Southworth-Anthoesen Press, 1941.

Rotella, Elyce J. "The Transformation of the American Office: Changes in Employment and Technology." *Journal of American History* 41 (1981): 51–57.

Siegel, Fred. "Artisans and Immigrants in the Politics of Late Antebellum Georgia." *Civil War History* 27 (1981): 221–30.

Sylvis, William H. "Letters from the South." In *Life, Speeches, Labors and Essays of William H. Sylvis*, edited by James C. Sylvis. New York: Augustus M. Kelley, 1968.

Van Kleeck, Mary. "Changes in Women's Work in Binderies." *Academy of Political Science. Proceedings* 1 (1910): 27–39.

Wiener, Jonathan M. "Class Structure and Economic Development in the American South, 1865–1955." *American Historical Review* 84 (1979): 970–1006.

## Published Sources: Books

*I. Primary Sources*

American Railway Master Mechanics Association. *Fifth Annual Report* (1872). Chicago: R. R. Donnelley & Sons, 1889.

Barnwell, V. T. *Barnwell's Atlanta City Directory and Strangers' Guide.* Atlanta: Intelligencer Book and Job Office, 1867.

*Beasley's Atlanta Directory for 1874.* Atlanta: Beasley & Co., n.d.

*Beasley's Atlanta Directory for 1875.* Atlanta: James W. Beasley, n.d.

Blassingame, John W., ed. *Slave Testimony: Two Centuries of Letters, Speeches, Interviews, and Autobiographies.* Baton Rouge: Louisiana State University Press, 1977.

Brotherhood of Locomotive Engineers. *Constitution and By-Laws of the Grand International Division.* Ft. Wayne, Ind.: Jones and Son, 1868.

Clarke, E. Y. *Atlanta Illustrated.* Atlanta: Jas. P. Harrison, 1881.

Colored National Labor Convention. *Proceedings.* Washington: New Era Printing Office, 1870.

Douglass, Frederick. *Narrative of the Life of Frederick Douglass, An American Slave.* Garden City, New York: Doubleday, 1963.

Foner, Philip S. and Ronald L. Lewis, eds. *The Black Worker: A Documentary History from Colonial Times to the Present.* Vol. 1: *The Black Worker to 1869.* Vol. 2: *The Black Worker in the Era of the National Labor Union.* Philadelphia: Temple University Press, 1978.

*Hanleiter's Atlanta City Directory for 1870.* Atlanta: William R. Hanleiter, 1870.

*Hanleiter's Atlanta City Directory for 1871.* Atlanta: William R. Hanleiter, 1871.

*Hanleiter's Atlanta City Directory for 1872.* Atlanta: Plantation Publishing Company, 1872.

Master Car-Builders of the United States. *Fourth Annual Report of the Master Car-Builders Association of the United States, in Convention at New York City.* New York, 1870.

National Archives Microfilm Publications. *Population Schedules of the Ninth Census of the United States, 1870.* Washington, 1965.

National Archives Microfilm Publications. *Population Schedules of the Tenth Census of the United States, 1880.* Washington, 1965.

*Norton's Directory of the City of Atlanta for 1879.* Atlanta: Charles Norton & Co., 1879.

Severance, Margaret. *Official Guide to Atlanta.* Atlanta: Foote and Davies, 1895.

*Sholes' Atlanta City Directory for 1877.* Atlanta: Sunny South Publishing House, n.d.

*Sholes' Directory of the City of Atlanta for 1878.* n.p.: A. E. Sholes, n.d.

*Sholes' Directory of the City of Atlanta for 1880.* Atlanta: A. E. Sholes, n.d.

*Sholes' Directory for the City of Atlanta for 1881.* Atlanta: H. H. Dickson, n.d.

Sinclair, Angus. *Locomotive Engine Running and Management: A Treatise on Locomotive Engines.* New York: John Wiley and Sons, 1886.

United States. Bureau of Labor. *Fifth Annual Report of the Commissioner of Labor, 1889: Railroad Labor.* Washington, 1890.

United States. Census Office. *Ninth Census (1870).* Vol. 3: *Statistics of the Wealth and Industry of the United States.* Washington, 1872.

United States. Census Office. *Tenth Census* (1880). Vol. 2: *Report on the Manufacturers of the United States.* Washington, 1883.

Western & Atlantic Railroad Company. *Annual Reports of the Officers of the Western & Atlantic Rail Road.* Atlanta: Atlanta Intelligencer Book & Job Office, 1866.

Western & Atlantic Railroad Company. *Annual Reports of the Officers of the Western & Atlantic Railroad* (1868). Atlanta: New Era Job Office, 1869.

Western & Atlantic Railroad Company. *Annual Reports of the Officers of the Western & Atlantic Railroad* (1869). Atlanta: Samuel Bard, 1870.

Wilson, John Stainback. *Atlanta As It Is: Being a Brief Sketch of Its Early Settlers, Growth, Society, Health, Morals, Publications, Churches, Associations, Educational Institutions, Prominent Officials, Principal Business Enterprises, Public Buildings, Etc., Etc.* New York: Little, Rennie & Co., 1871; reprinted as *Atlanta Historical Bulletin* 7, no. 24 (January/April 1941).

II. *Secondary Sources*

Andrews, Sidney. *The South Since the War.* New York: Arno Press and the New York Times, 1969.

Applebaum, Herbert A. *Royal Blue: The Culture of Construction Workers.* New York: Holt, Rinehart and Winston, 1981.

Ashworth, John H. *The Helper and American Trade Unions.* Baltimore: Johns Hopkins Press, 1915.

Avery, I. W. *The History of the State of Georgia from 1850 to 1881.* New York: Brown & Derby, 1881.

Baker, Elizabeth Faulkner. *Technology and Woman's Work.* New York: Columbia University Press, 1964.

Bartley, Numan V. *The Creation of Modern Georgia.* Athens: University of Georgia Press, 1983.

Beynon, Ross E. *Roll Design and Mill Layout.* Pittsburgh: Association of Iron and Steel Engineers, 1956.

Brody, David. *The Butcher Workmen: A Study of Unionization.* Cambridge: Harvard University Press, 1964.

———. *Steelworkers in America: The Nonunion Era.* New York: Harper Torchbooks, 1960.

Butler, Frank O. *The Story of Papermaking: An Account of Paper-Making From Its Earliest Known Record Down To the Present Time.* Chicago: J. W. Butler Paper Company, 1901.

Campbell, Sir George. *White and Black: The Outcome of a Visit to the United States.* New York: Negro Universities Press, 1979.

Carter, Edward R. *The Black Side: A Partial History of the Business, Religious, and Educational Side of the Negro in Atlanta, Georgia.* Atlanta: n.p., 1894.

Chandler, Alfred D., Jr. *The Visible Hand: The Managerial Revolution in American Business*. Cambridge and London: Belknap Press of Harvard University Press, 1977.

Clark, Victor S. *History of Manufactures in the United States*. 3 vols. Vol. 2: 1860-1893. New York: Peter Smith, 1949.

Clawson, Dan. *Bureaucracy and the Labor Process: The Transformation of U. S. Industry, 1860-1920*. New York and London: Monthly Review Press, 1980.

Coleman, Kenneth, ed. *A History of Georgia*. Athens: University of Georgia Press, 1977.

Cooper, Walter. *The Official History of Fulton County*. Atlanta: Walter G. Brown Publishing, 1934.

Dennett, John Richard. *The South As It Is: 1865-1866*. New York: Viking Press, 1965.

Dubofsky, Melvyn. *Industrialism and the American Worker, 1865-1920*. New York: Thomas Y. Crowell, 1975.

DuBois, W. E. B. *Black Reconstruction in America, 1860-1880*. New York: Atheneum, 1971.

DuBois, W. E. Burghardt, ed. *The Negro Artisan*. Atlanta: Atlanta University Press, 1902; reprinted., New York: Arno Press and the New York Times, 1969.

Dunbar, James. *Notes on the Manufacture of Wood Pulp and Wood-Pulp Paper*. Leith: MacKenzie & Storne, 1894.

Fink, Leon. *Workingmen's Democracy: The Knights of Labor and American Politics*. Urbana: University of Illinois Press, 1983.

Garrett, Franklin M. *Atlanta and Environs: A Chronicle of Its People and Events*. 2 vols. Athens: University of Georgia Press, 1969.

Goldfield, David R. *Cotton Fields and Skyscrapers: Southern City and Region, 1607-1980*. Baton Rouge and London: Louisiana State University Press, 1982.

Grossman, Jonathan Philip. *William Sylvis, Pioneer of American Labor: A Study of the Labor Movement During the Era of the Civil War*. New York: Octagon Books, 1973.

Gutman, Herbert G. *Work, Culture and Society in Industrializing America: Essays in American Working-Class and Social History*. New York: Vintage Books, 1976.

Hahn, Steven. *The Roots of Southern Populism: Yeoman Farmers and the Transformation of the Georgia Upcountry, 1850-1890*. New York and Oxford: Oxford University Press, 1983.

Harris, William H. *The Harder We Run: Black Workers Since the Civil War*. New York: Oxford University Press, 1982.

Hertzberg, Steven. *Strangers Within the Gate City: The Jews of Atlanta, 1845-1915*. Philadelphia: Jewish Publication Society of America, 1978.

Jaynes, Gerald David. *Branches Without Roots: Genesis of the Black Working Class in the American South, 1862-1882*. New York and Oxford: Oxford University Press, 1986.

Jones, Jacqueline. *Labor of Love, Labor or Sorrow: Black Women, Work, and the Family from Slavery to the Present*. New York: Basic Books, 1985.

Katzman, David M. *Seven Days A Week: Women and Domestic Service in Industrializing America*. Urbana: University of Illinois Press, 1978.

Kessler-Harris, Alice. *Out to Work: A History of Wage-Earning Women in the United States*. New York: Oxford Unversity Press, 1982.

BIBLIOGRAPHY / 125

Knight, Lucian Lamar. *History of Fulton County Georgia.* Atlanta: A. H. Cawston, 1930.

Kornweibel, Theodore, ed. *In Search of the Promised Land: Essays in Black Urban History.* Port Washington, N.Y.: Kennikat Press, 1981.

Laslett, John H. M. *Labor and the Left: A Study of Socialist and Radical Influences in the American Labor Movement, 1881–1924.* New York: Basic Books, 1970.

Licht, Walter. *Working for the Railroad: The Organization of Work in the Nineteenth Century.* Princeton: Princeton University Press, 1983.

Lightner, David L. *Labor on the Illinois Central Railroad, 1852–1900.* New York: Arno Press, 1977.

Litwack, Leon F. *Been in the Storm So Long: The Aftermath of Slavery.* New York: Vintage Books, 1979.

McLaurin, Melton Alonza. *The Knights of Labor in the South.* Westport, Conn.: Greenwood Press, 1978.

Matthaei, Julie A. *An Economic History of Women in America: Women's Work, The Sexual Division of Labor and the Development of Capitalism.* New York: Schocken Books, 1982.

Middletown, P. Harvey. *Railways and Organized Labor.* Chicago: Railway Business Association, 1941.

Montgomery, David. *Beyond Equality: Labor and the Radical Republicanism, 1862–1872.* New York: Vintage Books, 1967.

_____. *Workers' Control in America: Studies in the History of Work, Technology, and Labor Struggles.* New York: Cambridge University Press, 1979.

Northrup, Herbert R. *The Negro in the Paper Industry.* Philadelphia: Industrial Research Unit, Department of Industry, Wharton School of Finance and Commerce, University of Pennsylvania, 1969.

_____. *Organized Labor and the Negro.* New York and London: Harper and Brothers, 1944.

Panschar, William G. *Baking in America: Economic Development.* Evanston, Ill.: Northwestern University Press, 1956.

Quarles, Benjamin. *Frederick Douglass.* New York: Atheneum, 1968.

Rabinowitz, Howard. *Race Relations in the Urban South, 1865–1890.* Urbana: University of Illinois Press, 1980.

Rayback, Joseph G. *A History of American Labor.* New York: The Free Press, 1966.

Reagan, Alice E. *H. I. Kimball, Entrepreneur.* Atlanta: Cherokee Publishing Company, 1983.

Reed, Wallace P. *History of Atlanta, Georgia.* Syracuse, N.Y.: D. Mason & Co., 1889.

Richardson, Reed Cott. *The Locomotive Engineer, 1863–1963: A Century of Railway Labor Relations.* Ann Arbor: Bureau of Industrial Relations, Graduate School of Business Administration, University of Michigan, 1963.

Risher, Howard W., Jr. *The Negro in the Railroad Industry.* Philadelphia: Industrial Research Unit, Department of Industry, Wharton School of Finance and Commerce, University of Pennsylvania, 1971.

Robinson, Jesse S. *The Amalgamated Association of Iron, Steel and Tin Workers.* Baltimore: Johns Hopkins Press, 1920.

Rodgers, Daniel T. *The Work Ethic in Industrial America, 1850–1920.* Chicago and London: University of Chicago Press, 1978.

Salvatore, Nick. *Eugene V. Debs: Citizen and Socialist.* Urbana: University of Illinois Press, 1982.

Saxton, Alexander. *The Indispensable Enemy: Labor and the Anti-Chinese Movement in California.* Berkeley: University of California Press, 1971.

Spero, Sterling D. and Abram L. Harris. *The Black Worker: The Negro and the Labor Movement.* New York: Atheneum Press, 1974.

Starobin, Robert S. *Industrial Slavery in the Old South.* London: Oxford University Press, 1970.

Stockton, Frank T. *International Molders Union of North America.* Baltimore: Johns Hopkins Press, 1921.

Stone, Charles F. *The Story of Dixisteel: The First Fifty Years, 1901–1951.* Atlanta: Atlantic Steel Company, 1951.

Tilly, Louise A. and Charles Tilly, eds. *Class Conflict and Collective Action.* Beverly Hills: Sage Publications, 1981.

Todes, Charlotte. *William H. Sylvis and the National Labor Union.* New York: International Publishers, 1942.

Trachtenberg, Alan. *The Incorporation of America: Culture and Society in the Gilded Age.* New York: Hill and Wang, 1982.

Ulman, Lloyd. *The Rise of the National Trade Union: The Development and Significance of Its Structure, Governing Institutions, and Economic Policies.* Cambridge: Harvard University Press, 1955.

United States. Department of Labor. *Bulletin.* No. 22 (May, 1899): "The Negro in the Black Belt: Some Social Sketches," by W. E. B. DuBois. Washington, 1899.

United States. Department of Labor. *Bulletin of the United States Bureau of Labor Statistics.* No. 209: "Hygiene of the Printing Trades," by Alice Hamilton and Charles H. Verrill. Washington, 1917.

United States. Department of Labor. Women's Bureau. *Bulletin of the Women's Bureau.* No. 22: "Women in Georgia Industries: A Study of Hours, Wages, and Working Conditions." Washington, 1922.

Van Kleeck, Mary. *Women in the Bookbinding Trade.* New York: Survey Associates, 1913.

Wade, Richard C. *Slavery in the Cities: The South, 1820–1860.* New York: Oxford University Press, 1964.

Warren, Kenneth. *The American Steel Industry, 1850–1970: A Geographical Interpretation.* Oxford: Clarendon Press, 1973.

Wertheimer, Barbara Mayer. *We Were There: The Story of Working Women in America.* New York: Pantheon, 1977.

Woodward, C. Vann. *Origins of the New South, 1877–1913.* Baton Rouge: Louisiana State University Press, 1971.

Wright, Gavin. *Old South, New South: Revolutions in the Southern Economy Since the Civil War.* New York: Basic Books, 1986.

_____. *The Political Economy of the Cotton South: Households, Markets, and Wealth in the Nineteenth Century*. New York: W. W. Norton and Company, 1978.

Zimilies, Martha and Murray Zimilies. *Early American Mills*. New York: Clarkson N. Potter, 1973.

## Unpublished Sources

*I. Primary Sources*

American Missionary Association. Archives. Georgia Manuscript. Microfilm copy.

Bryant, John Emory. "Missionary Work Among the Destitute Whites At Atlanta, Ga." John Emory Bryant Papers, Duke University, The Perkins Library, Manuscripts Division.

Richards, Samuel P. "Diary." Atlanta Historical Society.

*II. Secondary Sources*

Evans, Mercer Griffin. "The History of the Organized Labor Movement in Georgia." Ph.D. dissertation, University of Chicago, 1929.

Flynn, Charles Lenean, Jr. "White Land, Black Labor: Property, Ideology, and the Political Economy of Late Nineteenth-Century Georgia." Ph.D. dissertation, Duke University, 1980.

Freifeld, Mary Ellen. "The Emergence of the American Working Classes: The Roots of Division, 1865–1885." Ph.D. dissertation, New York University, 1980.

Garlock, Jonathan Ezra. "A Structural Analysis of the Knights of Labor: A Prolegomenon to the History of the Producing Classes." Ph.D. dissertation, University of Rochester, 1974.

Hahn, Steven Howard. "The Roots of Southern Populism: Yeomen Farmers and the Transformation of Georgia's Upper Piedmont, 1850–1890." Ph.D. dissertation, Yale University, 1979.

Henson, Stephen Ray. "Industrial Workers in the Mid Nineteenth-Century South: Atlanta Railwaymen, 1840–1870." Ph.D. dissertation, Emory University, 1982.

Hopkins, Richard Joseph. "Patterns of Persistence and Occupational Mobility in a Southern City: Atlanta, 1870–1920." Ph.D. dissertation, Emory University, 1972.

Huffman, Frank Jackson. "Old South, New South: Continuity and Change in a Georgia County, 1850–1880." Ph.D. dissertation, Yale University, 1974.

Janiewski, Dolores Elizabeth. "From Field to Factory: Race, Class, Sex, and the Woman Worker in Durham, 1880–1940." Ph.D. dissertation, Duke University, 1979.

Licht, Walter Martin. "Nineteenth-Century American Railwaymen: A Study in the Nature and Organization of Work." Ph.D. dissertation, Princeton University, 1977.

McLeod, Jonathan Woolard. "Black and White Workers: Atlanta During Reconstruction." Ph.D. dissertation, University of California, Los Angeles, 1987.

Matthews, John Michael. "Studies in Race Relations in Georgia, 1890–1930." Ph.D. dissertation, Duke University, 1970.

Robbins, Edwin Clyde. "Railway Conductors: A Study in Organized Labor." Ph.D. dissertation, Columbia University, 1914.

Russell, James Michael. "Atlanta: Gate City of the South, 1847 to 1885." Ph.D. dissertation, Princeton University, 1972.

Taylor, Arthur Reed. "From the Ashes: Atlanta During Reconstruction, 1865–1876." Ph.D. dissertation, Emory University, 1973.

Thornbery, Jerry John. "The Development of Black Atlanta, 1865–1885." Ph.D. dissertation, University of Maryland, 1977.

Wingo, Horace Calvin. "Racial Relations in Georgia, 1872–1908." Ph.D. dissertation, University of Georgia, 1969.

Wotton, Grigsby Hart, Jr. "New City of the South: Atlanta, 1843–1873." Ph.D. dissertation, Johns Hopkins University, 1973.

# Index

African-American culture, 103
Age divisions, in smaller-scale industries, 78
Agricultural implements manufacturing, 10, 76–77
Agriculture: declining price structure of, in Georgia, 57; effect on railroad industry, 64n. 12
Alabama, iron manufacturing in, 9
Albert, Thomas, a black skilled molder, 45–46
Amalgamated Association of Iron and Steel Workers (the Amalgamated), 46, 51; Atlanta Lodge formed, 52; broadening of union base, 49–50; strike of 1881, 54, 60
Atlanta: Atlanta City Council, 98, 103; Civil War destruction, 1, 7, 8, 42, 56; former names of, 5; limited potential for iron production in, 54; police, 98, 103; population, 1, 102; rebuilding and expansion, 15–16, 75, 94; as Southern railroading center, 30–31; Summerhill neighborhood, 103. See also Economy of Atlanta
Atlanta & Charlotte Airline Railroad, 8
Atlanta & West Point Railroad, 5, 25
Atlanta Cotton Factory, 11, 84–85, 87
Atlanta Masonic Lodge, No. 59, 32
Atlanta Rolling Mill, 12, 16, 73; craft unions and workers'-control struggles, 50–55, 115; deskilling, 44–45, 48, 54; financial difficulties of, 44–45, 51; fire at, 44, 49, 55; history of, 6, 8–10, 67n. 57; labor force composition, 45, 55, 61; labor-management relations, 50–53, 115; labor market, 9, 42, 44; production relations, 21–22; promotion policy, 45, 53; skill division, 21, 47, 48–49, 62–63; strikes and job actions, 9, 49, 50, 51–53, 54–55, 60; wages, 47, 51–52, 54, 58; "yellow-dog" contracts, 51, 52, 115
Atlanta Typographical Union, No. 48 (ATU), 79
Augusta, textile mills in, 16

Bakeries, 88, 91
Barbers, 16
Barber shops, 13, 14
Benefits, employee, 37, 39
Bennetts, David, on blacks in printing and bookbinding, 78
Biracial unionism, ideal of, 106
Birmingham, iron and steel manufacturing in, 9, 45
Black churches, endorsement of washerwomen's strike, 103
Black-owned businesses: boot and shoe factories, 81; newspapers, 79; service sector ventures, 14–15
Black women workers: commercial laundry workers, 102; in domestic service, 101, 111n. 87; hotels, 100; needle trades, 81–82, 83; paper box manufacturing, 88; as slaves in iron manufacturing, 57; washerwomen, 102–3. See also Women workers
Black workers: attitudes towards white workers, 58–59; in construction, 94–95, 97, 98–99; cotton textile manufacturing, 85; craft unions, excluded from, 40–41, 46, 59, 62–63; in food processing, 91, 92, 93; in hotels and food service, 100; laborers in smaller foundries, 61; lumber and paper mills, 75; NLU, admission to, 105–6; organization into separate locals and "local option," 79–80, 99, 105–6; in printing and publishing, 78–80; in railroading, 24, 26, 28, 29, 31, 33–35, 40, 64–65n. 18; Republicans, 24, 106; in rolling and iron mills, 45–47, 50, 54–55, 56; seen competitively by white workers, 34, 56–58, 59–60, 63, 116; in service sector jobs, 14–15; in skilled positions, 26, 28, 45–46, 55, 58, 59, 91, 94, 97; as strikebreakers, 54, 60, 63, 98, 105. See also Racial divisions; Slaves
Blodgett, Foster, 7
Bookbinding, 77–79

16; black workers, 24, 34, 35; employment, 8, 22, 24; job actions against, 35, 36, 40, 41, 116; journeymen's helpers, 28-29; paternalism, 33; wages, 24-25, 32-33, 35

West Virginia, industry in, 16

White supremacy, 40

Wilkins, Grant, 52, 54-55

Willimantic Linen Company, 11

Wilson, Charles, 37

Winship, Joseph, 6, 61

Women workers: in bakeries, 91; barred from ITU membership, 79-80; candy production, 91-92; clerical sector, 13, 14; clothing manufacturing, 82, 83-84; cotton textile mills, 11, 84-85, 87; mobilization of, 114; and the NLU, 105, 106; in paper box manufacturing, 88; in printing and bookbinding, 78; retail sales clerks, 14, 104; shoe manufacturing, 80; straw goods manufacturing, 87. See also Black women workers

Workers' control, 113; meat packers, 94; railroad workers, 28, 35; rolling and iron mill workers, 50-55, 115; in smaller foundries, 62

Working-class communities, 5; railroad workers, 21, 40; rolling and iron mill workers, 21, 55, 56; studies on, 1, 55

Working-class consciousness and culture, 21, 113; agricultural implements manufacturing, 77; construction workers, 97;

planing mill workers, 76; railroad workers, 21, 32, 35, 39, 62, 113; rolling and iron mill workers, 21, 59, 60, 62

Working-class unity: biracial, 115, 116; railroad workers, 36, 38, 40

Working conditions, 1, 57; clothing manufacturing, 84; construction, 98; cotton textile manufacturing, 85, 87; of iron molders, 48; meat processing, 93; printing and bookbinding, 79; straw goods manufacturing, 87-88. See also Occupational safety

Workingmen's Union, No. 1, 35

Workplace: control of, 1; dynamics of, 21, 61

Work process, 1, 2, 11, 21, 113, 114, 115; of black domestic workers, 101; changed through mechanization, 78; in clothing manufacturing, 83, 84; construction, 95, 97; cotton textile manufacturing, 85; meat processing, 93; printing and bookbinding, 78; railroads, 22, 26, 30, 35; rolling and iron mills, 44-45, 47-49, 50, 51, 52, 54, 55, 59; service industries, 99; shoe manufacturing, 80; washerwomen and commerical laundry workers, 102

Wright, Austin, 34

"Yellow dog contracts," 51, 52, 115

Zimilies, Martha and Murray, on iron molders' work, 48